ACTA UNIVERSITATIS UPSA
Studia Doctrinae Christianae Up.
25

Carl Reinhold Bråkenhielm

Problems
of
Religious Experience

UPPSALA 1985

Distributed by:
Almqvist & Wiksell International
Stockholm – Sweden

Printed with a grant from The Swedish Council for Research in the Humanities and
Social Sciences

ISBN 91-554-1657-8
ISSN 0585-508X

Bråkenhielm, C. R. Problems of Religious Experience. Acta Universitatis
Upsaliensis. *Studia Doctrinae Christianae Upsaliensia* 25. 158 pp. Uppsala
1985. ISBN 91-554-1657-8.

Abstract
Are religious experiences illusions? Or are (at least some) religious experiences veridical? This is a
philosophical problem of great importance for theology. A central thesis in the present essay
is—negatively—that religious experiences are not self-authenticating and—positively—that they
require the backing of an overall world-view. In addition some guidelines for distinguishing true
religious experiences from false ones are required. These matters are dealt with in chapter 8–10.
However, various other problems of religious experience has to be solved first. Some of the most
important ones are discussed in chapter 1–7.

Chapter 1 focuses upon the concept of religious experience, which is explained in terms of
experiences of transcendence. Chapter 2 examines some arguments for the claim that religious
experiences cannot be conceptualized and concludes that some general concepts can be applied
even if the possibility of their revision remains permanently open. Chapter 3 scrutinizes some
arguments against the claim that experiences of God are possible. In chapter 4 the concept of
revelatory experiences is analysed and the possibility of a rational assessment of revelation-claims
discussed. In chapter 5 it is argued that the valid claim that religious experiences are determined by
underlying religious beliefs does not imply that religious experiences are without epistemological
significance. In chapter 6 a number of arguments against the veridicality of religious experiences is
examined. Chapter 7 contains a more extensive discussion on the epistemological consequences of
a natural explanation of religious experiences. It is argued that religious experiences can be
veridical experiences of the transcendent even if they have a natural explanation.

*Carl Reinhold Bråkenhielm, Department of Theology, Uppsala University, Box 1604, S-751 46
Uppsala, Sweden.*

ISBN 91-554-1657-8
ISSN 0585-508X

Printed in Sweden by
Graphic Systems AB, Göteborg 1985

To my children,
Maria and Carl Fredrik

Contents

Preface

This book contains some material which is presented (in Swedish) in other contexts. A shorter version of chapter 3 is published in *Filosofisk tidskrift 2, 1985*. I am indebted to the editor—Prof. Lars Bergström—for the possibility to publish the material in a more extensive version here. The main part of chapter 6 was held as a public lecture at the Faculty of Theology in Uppsala 1981. Chapter 7 derives largely from a lecture held at the Faculty of Theology in Lund and subsequently published in *Religionsfilosofiska perspektiv* (1983).

The Swedish Council for Research in the Humanities and Social Sciences has provided me with a grant which made it possible to print this book. I am deeply indebted to them as well as to the board of *Acta Universitatis Upsaliensis* and, particularly, to Prof. Anders Jeffner, who has given me the opportunity to publish the book in *Studia Doctrinae Christianae Upsaliensia*. Prof. Jeffner has also been a constant source of intellectual inspiration far beyond what the references to his works in this essay suggest. Needless to say, any shortcomings of this present book are entirely my own.

Dr Sten Philipson and Dr Johan Unger—two collegues and close friends—have been invaluable partners in dialogue during the years. They deserve many thanks.

Craig McKay has had the arduous task of correcting my English. The rawmaterial I gave him set certain limits to what could be done. I appreciate the help he has given me.

Anne-Marie Nilsson has typed the manuscript and Elsa Söderqvist has helped me to read the proofs. I am grateful for all their work.

I dedicate this book to my two children, Maria and Carl Fredrik. They have often asked what my work really amounts to. Well, this book is the most honest answer I can give them.

My wife, Ingalill, has given me all the time I needed for the work—even if it is questionable whether the project deserved all her generosity. For this and for many other things I am deeply grateful.

Introduction

When Swedish television recently gave a play about a man going through an intense religious experience, a critic dryly remarked: "The soul is not so easily photographed". He might have added ". . . and not so easily spoken about either". It may be the case that for most of us reality from time to time takes on certain religious qualities—yet, distinctive religious experiences are rather rare. But even if we were to come across a lot of these strange flowers of human existence—as, for example, William James did—their fugative and private character easily defies our analytical skill, not to mention the skill of the camera-man.

Nevertheless, the effort has been made by a considerable number of thinkers. This book is a study of some of these efforts made by theologians and philosophers. To illuminate the character of the present study a distinction between two kinds of studies concerning the thinking about religious experience could be made: *system-oriented studies* and *problem-oriented studies*. The difference between these two kind of studies is also suggested by Frederick Copleston in the preface to his latest volume of his *A History of Philosophy* (vol 9, part I). He speaks of "taking philosophers in succession and treating the thought of each as one block" on the one hand, and "treating the development of philosophical thought in terms of problems and themes" on the other hand.[1] An elaboration of this distinction will enable us to make the character of the present study more precise.

System-oriented studies can be classified from different points of view. One such point of view concerns the number of systems analyzed. A more interesting principle of division, however, concerns the nature of the relationships which are studied. One type (A) of system-oriented studies may focus upon the *internal relationships* of one or more systems of thought. Such studies are concerned with the logical structure of (for example) philosophical or theological systems. Such system-oriented studies may also be supplemented with a critical evaluation of the coherence of the system(s) and its (their) validity. An example of a system-oriented study of some theories of religious experience focused upon their logical structure and supplemented with critical considerations is John Morrison Moore's *Theories of Religious Experience with Special Reference to James, Otto and Bergson.*[2]

Another type of system-oriented study (B) is exemplified by those which have their focus upon the external relationships between the system(s) on the one hand and its (their) intellectual context—or more broadly with political and social circumstances. Such studies pay special attention to the influence of ideas from outside sources upon system(s) of thought. One may here be reminded of the special character of Bertrand Russell's history of philosophy, which is reflected in the title of his work: *History of Western Philosophy and its Connection with Political and Social Circumstances from the Earliest Times to the Present Day.*[3] A more central example within the field of this study is, however, Endre V Ivanka's work *Plato Christianus. Übernahme und Umgestaltung des Platonismus durch die Väter.*[4] But it must be observed that it is more concerned with the *intellectual* tradition of platonism and neoplatonism and its impact upon the thinking of the Fathers.

Lastly, we may discern a third category (C) which represents studies trying to combine the aims of A and B. An example of such a system-oriented study is the work of Gösta Wrede: *Unio Mystica. Probleme der Erfahrung bei Johannes Tauler.*[5] This study combines a detailed analysis of Tauler's theory of mysticism with a thorough investigation into the sources of his thinking. The accent of the study is, however, mainly upon description and not so much upon evaluation of the coherence and validity of Tauler's theory.

Let us now turn to problem-oriented studies. The object of interest is here not upon a system of thought, but rather upon the solution of a set of problems. The present study is of such a character. It is concerned with problems of religious experience. Needless to say, it would be presumptuous and foolish to deal with all problems which arise in connection with the phenomena called "religious experience". In this study, we shall limit ourselves to some *philosophical problems concerning religious experience.* We are not concerned with religious experience as a psychological problem, nor with the more specific problems which arise in connection with the detailed development of Christian doctrines. Nevertheless, many of the problems with which we are going to deal are of central relevance both to psychology and theology.

What kind of problems of religious experience can be counted as "philosophical" problems? Broadly, it could be said that philosophical problems of religious experience are a mixture of conceptual and epistemological problems. Philosophical problems arise because the language we use to describe the significance of such phenomena is puzzling. This calls for conceptual clarification. And even if those problems are overcome there is another set of problems to be faced by the philosopher, namely the epistemological evaluation of religious experiences: are religious experiences experiences of something real—or are they illusions?

Against the background of this broad description, it is possible to discern at least ten different philosphical problems of religious experience. Needless to say, the list could be made longer (but not—I would argue—very much longer). Nevertheless, the following problems are significant within the area we have delimited:

11

1 What is the nature of religious experience?

Various phenomena come to us under the description of religious experience. They range from refined mystical experiences to crude experiences of demons and angels. But not all of these experiences are of equal interest from an epistemological point of view. Is it possible to delimit and organize the area in some reasonable way? This problem is discussed in chapter 1.

2 Is it possible to conceptualize religious experiences?

When we consider the first problem about the nature of religous experience, we presuppose that it is possible to describe the content of religious experiences. But is this really possible? Many mystics have claimed that their religious experiences are ineffable. In chapter 2 we shall discuss some of the arguments which have been put forward to support this claim.

3 Are experiences of God possible?

If we assume that it makes sense to conceptualize religious experiences, we might still doubt the possibility of describing them as experiences of God. Do we normally use the word "experience" in such a way that it is possible to speak of experiences of God, i.e. God as God is conceived in the Judeo-Christian tradition? Chapter 3 is devoted to this problem.

4 What is the nature and significance of revelatory experiences?

For some people, experiences of God are quite unproblematic. But they find the idea of experiencing a revelation from God difficult and obscure. Needless to say, not all religious experiences are revelatory experiences. Further, not all relevatory experiences contain truths that are taken to be essential for the salvation of humanity. But some revelatory experiences are taken to have such a universal significance—it is at least part of Christian faith. But how are we to understand the nature of these experiences—and how are we to know if they are veridical or not? These problems will be taken up in chapter 4.

5 What is the relationship between religious experience and religious belief?

Problems 1–4 are of particular interest to the theologian only if the religious experiences in question can serve as evidence for a certain religious belief. But is this not to misunderstand the character of religious experience? Is it not more reasonable to conceive of religious belief as giving religious experience its character, than to take religious experiences as evidence for religious belief? This issue will be discussed in chapter 5.

6 Is the whole realm of religious experience an illusion?

We can take religious experience as evidence for certain certain religious beliefs only if these experiences are veridical. But many philosophers and theologians have argued that the whole realm of religious experiences has to be distrusted from an epistemological point of view. But what kind of arguments can be put forward to justify such a negative assessment of religious experience in general? Some of these arguments are discussed in chapter 6.

7 Are natural explanations of religious experience relevant for an epistemological evaluation of such experiences?

It is often suggested that if a natural explanation of religious experiences could be found, then it follows that religious experiences are illusory. Marx, Freud and Durkheim have suggested that such explanations can be found. We might feel unconvinced by their specific theories. But the philosophical problem remains: would a natural explanation of religious experiences show that these experiences are without cognitive content? This problem is discussed in chapter 7.

8 Are there self-authenticating religious experiences?

Natural explanations of religious experiences might leave the cognitive character of religious experiences undecided. But is there any positive reason to regard any religious experience as veridical? Some philosophers and theologians have argued that the solution to this problem lies in the idea of self-authenticating religious experience. But is such an idea coherent? And if it is — is it possible to know which experiences are self-authenticating and which are not? Chapter 8 is concerned with these issues.

9 What is the relevance of methaphysical reflection to the epistemological evaluation of religious experience?

When theologians speak of religious experience (for example Schleiermacher), they often do so as part of an effort to escape the cold rationality of metaphysical theology. Yet, the question can be asked if metaphysics *must* be an enemy of religious experience. Could it not be the case that it is—in some sense of the word—an ally? Is it possible that metaphysics is of central importance not only for defending the veridicality of religious experience, but also for the more detailed understanding of these experiences? These issues are discussed in chapter 9.

10 What are the criteria by which veridical religious experiences can be distinguished?

A metaphysical world-view might give us reason to reject those who claim that the whole realm of religious experience is illusory. But we are still faced with the task to distinguish genuine religious experiences from spurious ones. What criteria can be found for this purpose and what is the status of these criteria? This problem will be discussed in the final chapter of this essay (chapter 10).

As I said above there are other problems of religious experience which can be described as "philosophical". But the ten problems chosen for consideration are—I would argue—of central importance from a philosophical point of view.

Two other things must be said at the outset of this essay. First, this is not a book about the phenomenology of religious experience. It does not contain any extensive reports of religious experiences. Needless to say, aquaintance with such reports—or personal experiences—are necessary to appreciate the arguments in this essay. But the reader is advised to consult other books for such knowledge. William James' book on *The Varieties of religious Experience*[6] belongs to the classics, but it is still an invaluable source. F C Happold's book *Mysticism. A Study and an Anthology*[7] can also be recommended. It contains many influential reports of religious experiences from both east and west. David Hay's book *Exploring Inner Space*[8] and Michael Cox' introduction to the Christian mystical tradition (*Mysticism. The direct experience of God*[9]) are of a more popular character, but still of value as a background to the philosophical analysis in the present essay.

It must also be underlined that these problems of religious experience are discussed within a special context, namely the contemporary discussion between philosophical theologians within the English-speaking world. This study is not a study which sufficiently mirrors the discussion about these problems in other parts of the world. Nevertheless, I think it is defensible to delimit the study in the way I have done. The problems which will be discussed in this study have mainly been studied by philosophical theologians in the English-speaking world.

NOTES

[1] See Copleston 1977, p. 11.
[2] Moore 1938.
[3] Russell 1967.
[4] Ivanka 1964.
[5] Wrede 1974.
[6] James 1974.
[7] Happold 1971.
[8] Hay 1982.
[9] Cox 1983.

Chapter 1

The nature of religious experience

"The over-all impression is of the immense diversity of religious experiences".[1] This remark by Ronald Hepburn contains a great deal of truth. And when William James choose the title *Varieties of Religious Experience* for his famous book he expressed a similar insight. Further the contention has been corroborated by recent empirical studies in the field.[2]

Yet the title of this study—and numerous others—suggest that there exists a certain set of characteristics which distinguishes the phenomena of religious experiences from other phenomena. We shall return to this question below. But whether or not we are essentialists when it comes to religious experience, we could nevertheless agree that there are certain things which we ought to keep in mind when we approach this variegated field. I will begin this chapter by giving some general remarks about religious experience. Secondly, I shall make an effort to define the expression "religious experience". And, thirdly, I shall discuss different divisions of the phenomena delimited by the proposed definition.

Some general remarks concerning religious experience

First of all it is important to note that *religious experience* is an abstract concept in the sense that it invites us to think of the phenomena denoted by the expression in a way that detaches the phenomena from (a) the context in which they appear, (b) the person which has the experience, (c) the particular content of the experience and (d) the specific consequences of the experience. The idea of religious experience is an abstraction—and it has the usefulness and disadvantage which characterizes abstractions in general. Abstractions enhance the capacity of the mind—but abstractions may also blind us to import differences. There are different remedies for such an intellectual corruption. We may reject the abstraction altogether—or limit its use to a specified set of phenomena. When it comes to the concept of religious experience it seems clear that one of these remedies must be chosen. In the present study, we shall try to limit the use of the expression in such a way that it can serve as an important tool at least in the context of the present study. But this makes it necessary to make four important distinctions.

1 Intentional – nonintentional experiences

We must pay attention to the fact that the heterogeneous field of religious experience does not only contain experiences which are intentional. By "intentional experiences" I mean experiences which point beyond themselves to something which exists independently of the experience.[3] Many experiences lack this property of intentionality. They do not suggest the existence of anything beyond the experience. Feelings of joy and sadness are (sometimes) nonintentional experiences. But when I experience the trees outside my window I have experiences which are intentional.

In a similar manner we may say that many—but not all—religious experiences are intentional. Many people have experiences of the presence of God. These experiences are usually intentional. Other people have no experiences of God; but at some times they may have a feeling of peace or even bliss. These feelings are often nonintentional.

We must observe that even if an experience is nonintentional, it is not necessarily the case that this experience gives us no knowledge. Some philosophers have even argued that the most important truths about human nature can be detected through nonintentional feelings. Kierkegaard and Heidegger took the feeling of anxiety as the most important "symptom" of the freedom of human beings.[4] The justification for taking such feelings as a clue to important truths of human nature are far from clear. In any case we should avoid saying that those feelings—or any other feelings—are intentional, if they do not *within themselves* contain a perspicuous element which points beyond the experience to something which exists independently of the experience.[5]

2 Propositional – nonpropositional experiences

Roderick Chisholm has drawn attention to the fact that experiential terms are sometimes used in propositional way and sometimes in a nonpropositional way. When we use an experiential term (such as "observe", "hear", "feel" etc.) in a propositional way, then it is also possible to say that we have some kind of knowledge *that*. But when we use an experiential term in a non-propositional way this is not possible. Chisholm illustrates his distinction with a passage from *Robinson Crusoe*:

"When, one morning the day broke, and all unexpectedly before their eyes a ship stood, what it was was evident at a glance to Crusoe . . . But how was it with Friday? As younger and uncivilized his eyes were presumably better than those of his master. That is, Friday saw the ship really the best of the two; and yet he could hardly be said to see it at all." Using "see" nonpropositionally, we may say that Friday not only saw the ship, but saw it better than Crusoe did; using it propositionally, we may say that Crusoe, but not Friday, saw *that* it was a ship and hence, that Friday hardly saw a ship at all.[6]

Friday was, presumably, "stunned" by the sight of the ship. With C.D. Broad we could say that his experience had an "absence of aboutness".[7] Whereas Crusoe's experience involved a clear judgement *about* that which he saw, Friday's experience did not contain any judgement at all.

This distinction can be applied in the field of religious experience. Some religious experiences come close to the nonpropositional type. They are experiences of "das ganz Andere", which eludes all judgement (whether or not some judgement is still involved, let alone possible, will be the theme of the next chapter). Most religious experiences, however, seem to involve some kind of judgement. But it is of great importance to observe that there are basically two kinds of judgements involved in those religious experiences— and in propositional experiences in general. First, there are those judgements which do not go beyond the content of the experience. Secondly, there are those judgements which go beyond the content of the experience. We may call the first type of judgements *noninterpretative judgements* (and the experiences involving such judgements noninterpretative experiences) and the second type *interpretative judgements* (interpretative experiences).[8] It is not easy to make this distinction exact, but we might say that even if both noninterpretative and interpretative experiences can be erroneous, it is possible for interpretative experiences to be erroneous in a way that noninterpretative experiences cannot. Let me take an example: I have had many experiences of a chestnut-tree outside my window. If somebody with knowledge of biology were to tell me that my experiences have been erroneous because the tree in question is not a chestnut-tree but a lime-tree, I would be surprised but admit that there was nothing in my experience which should have made me experience the tree as a chestnut-tree in the first place. When my illusion concerning the tree outside my window breaks down, I recognize the (false) interpretative judgement in my former experiences. But a similar mistake would not have been possible, if my experiences had been simply experiences of a tree. Those experiences would have contained only noninterpretative judgements.

(Some philosophers have argued that *all* experience of physical objects, other minds or God are interpretative experiences. Experiences of external objects do always involve a judgement about something which does not belong to the content of the experiences. Such judgements must be based upon experiences which *only* involve noninterpretative judgements. These experiences have sometimes been described as sense-data. It has often been presup-

19

posed that experiences of external things cannot be described as noninterpretative experiences. But there is reason to question this presupposition—as G. J. Warnock does in an introduction to Berkeley: "... we do not have to agree either with Locke or Berkeley *unless* we accept, as they both did, the initial supposition that in perception we are aware *only* of 'our own ideas'. . ."[9])

Against the background of these remarks it is possible to say two important things about propositional religious experiences in general. First, that a religious experience is veridical, when the judgement involved in the experience is true. If the experience is noninterpretative, this means that person makes a true judgement about the content of his or her experience—and nothing else. If the experience is interpretative, then it means that the person makes a correct judgement about something which does not belong to the experience only. Certain experiences may involve both noninterpretative and interpretative judgements. If these judgements have a religious content and if some of these religious judgements are true, then we might still say that the experience is veridical (even if it, in reality, is only partially veridical).

Secondly, the fact that religious experiences often involve judgements, does not imply a denial of the claim that there exists one or many psychological universals in the religious experience of mankind. A psychological universal is a basic psychological process which constitutes the core of many different human experiences as they appear in various historical and cultural situations. The existence of such psychological universals of religious experience have been defended by Friedrich Schleiermacher, Rudolf Otto and Walter Stace. They have argued that there is a kind of nonpropositional religious experience at the core of seemingly different religious experiences. The whole idea of such psychological universals has recently been rejected by Steven Katz.[10] As will be obvious in chapter 6 I am more convinced by the arguments for the existence of certain psychological universals in religion than by the arguments for the opposite view.

The process of judgement within—or in connection with—religious experiences has been claimed to resemble the process of interpretation in ordinary sensual perception. John Hick (who does not make a clear distinction between noninterpretative and interpretative religious experiences) has described the interpretative activity of the perceiving mind as "an unconscious and habitual process, the process by which a sense-field is perceived, for example, as a three-dimensional room, or a particular configuration of coloured patches within that field as a book lying upon a table."[11] Analogically religious faith can be understood as "an interpretation of the world as a whole as mediating a divine presence and purpose".[12] This analogy between sense experience and religious experience may have its limits (which has been pointed out by—for example—Terence Penelhum and Vincent Brümmer). Nevertheless, it is an approach which is fruitful for the analysis of many—but not all—religious experiences.

3 Internal – external descriptions of experiences

A distinction must be made between the fact that a person, A, has a certain experience, e, and the fact that e is an experience of something real. In other words: it may be a fact that A has an e; but this does not always make it a fact that e is an experience of something real. Hallucinations and illusions are experiences—but they are not experiences of something real. It is controversial in what category we should put religious experiences. As a consequence of this, we should avoid a delimitation of the phenomena of religious experiences, which presupposes an answer to this question.

This distinction could be further explained by distinguishing—as Richard Swinburne does[13]—between an internal and an external description of religious experiences. Swinburne gives the following example. "Hearing a coach outside my window" is an external description of my experience. It follows from this description that there is a coach outside my window. But "having an auditory sensation which seemed to come from a coach outside the window" does not entail the existence of anything external of which the experience was purportedly an experience (or its nonexistence). An *internal description* does not presuppose that the experience is veridical. But *an external description* of the experience does entail the existence of the intentional object of the experience.

4 Direct – indirect experiences

We should finally make another distinction between those experiences in which there is no difference between the experiencing subject and the experienced object on the one hand, and experiences where there is such a difference. Experiences of the first type—direct experiences—are reported from many field outside religion (for example sexual experiences and experiences of unity with nature). But they are especially characteristic of the mystics in the Eastern religions. Some of them tell us that they have had a unitative experience in which their self has merged with ultimate reality leaving nothing inbetween.

Most experiences—and most religious experiences—are indirect. This means that there is a difference between the subject and the object and a chain of intermediates whereby the object affects the subject. Despite this chain of intermediates (such as light, electrical currents, nerve fibres etc.) we may nevertheless say that we experience the object provided that the intermediates do not significantly distort the qualities of the object.[14] We may even say that the experiences of objects through intermediates are direct, but not in the sense of *ontologically* direct. These experiences are, rather, *psychologically* direct. They have the quality of what George Mavrodes has called "psychological immediacy" which can be contrasted with the mediacy of reflective inference.[15]

Some mystics claim that in their religious experience there are no intermediates. But at least in some cases it could be argued that some intermediates are still present, even if some of the usual intermediates are absent.[16] This fact could account for the extraordinary character of at least some mystical experiences. Let me take a familiar analogy: if I often read about a person and then suddenly meet him or her face to face, I have a strong experience of psychological directness—even if there are still intermediates present between that person and my experience of him or her.

Let us now—against the background of these general remarks—look into the possibility of delimiting the vast field of religious experiences. We shall begin with a specific definition.

Religious experiences as experiences of the supernatural

In his book *The Existence of God,* Richard Swinburne suggest that the class of phenomena to be called "religious experience" could be delimited by the following definition:

> For our present purposes it will be useful to define it as an experience which seems (epistemically) to the subject to be an experience of God (either of his just being there, or doing or bringing about something) or some other supernatural thing.[17]

There are at least seven things which must be noted about this definition of religious experience.

1. It is clear that Swinburne delimits the phenomena of religious experience from the perspective of a particular purpose. This purpose could broadly be characterized as epistemological. I think that this procedure is justified and that the purpose coincides largely with the purpose of the present study. But it must not be forgotten that many phenomena which have been called "religious experience" are left out of a definition made for the purpose of coming to grips

with the epistemological problem of religious experience. In addition many of the experiences outside such a definition may be of central importance to a particular religion.

Swinburne proposes an abstract definition. As we said earlier, abstract definitions which radically detach religious experiences from their context should be avoided. This means that religious experiences should be delimited not only with reference to their content, but also (if possible) with reference to their function. I shall return to this problem below.

2. If we look at the content of Swinburne's definition, there are several things to be noted. We could make a distinction between definitions which treat religious experiences as certain isolated events at a particular place and a particular time and definitions which are more field-oriented. Swinburne's definition belongs to the former category. But many philosophers have underlined that religious experience could also be understood as referring to a broader context. Consider the following quotation by Stewart Sutherland on St. Paul's experience on his way to Damascus:

> In showing what significance the various parts of his life had St. Paul was showing what the significance of his experience was. To understand that—the significance of the experience—is to understand why Paul preached as he did; why he argued that the Law was in itself insufficient; why he travelled throughout Asia Minor as he did; how it was that he was able to suffer as he did without loosing his faith. If all this is true, then to understand what a religious experience is, what the significance of *this* experience is, which is what makes it religious, is not possible solely on the basis of attention to the moment of experience and Saul's psychological state at that moment.[18]

Sutherland's important remark notwithstanding, I would still claim that we have need for a concept of religious experience which treats religious experience as an event which occurs at a certain place and at a certain time. This dateable character may or may not be of importance for the person who has the experience. Still we need some kind of concept to describe extraordinary experiences which people sometimes have in certain situations. Possibly, we should avoid abstracting the content of these experiences from the subsequent response of the person having the experience. But some reference to a particular psychological event seems necessary.

3. Swinburne's definition restricts the phenomena of religious experience to those experiences which are taken to point beyond themselves to something other than the experience. In other words: according to Swinburne's definition all religious experiences are intentional experiences. It seems to be reasonable

delimitation of the area. Nonintentional experience may be of importance in religion, but when it comes to the epistemological evaulation of religious experiences, then the focus is upon intentional religious experiences.

It should however be noted that certain experiences are open to different judgements about their intentionality—some people would judge an experience of peace as an experience which does not point beyond itself, while others might judge a similar experience as an experience of the peace of God which passeth all understanding. George Mavrodes has pointed out that certain nonintentional experiences may serve as "signs" of the presence of some other sort of fact. A diabetic could take a certain buzzing in the ears as a sign of an approaching attack. And a believer might take feelings of bliss and peace as "signs" of the presence of God.[19] For other people similar experiences are not taken as intentional in a similar manner.

It is difficult to determine if a definition or religious experience should apply to only those religious experiences which contain *within themselves a salient reference to something beyond the experience* or if the definition should be broadened to include also experiences which contain no such element but which nevertheless could be judged (rightly or wrongly) as being intentional. In the present context I am inclined to follow Swinburne. A broader definition would include religious experiences which raise specific epistemological problems, which are of another character than the problems of clearly intentional experiences. In the present context I shall limit myself to a discussion raised by those experiences only.

4. Swinburne's definition is exclusively concentrated upon the *content* of religious experiences. He does not make any reference to the particular *function* of religious experiences. This results in an unnecessarily abstract definition. Furthermore, our normal use of the expression "religious experience" seems to imply something about the emotional impact of the experience. Some thinkers are inclined to stress this personal function of religious experiences. Arthur Danto speaks of *mystical* experiences, but the following statement is nevertheless worth quoting in the present context.

> It would hardly seem a mystical experience, if it did not alter *everything*: facts, values, attitudes and, most profoundly the entire categorical structures which define common experience.[20]

I think that Danto goes a bit too far. If we were to chose his line of argument, then we would arrive at a very narrow definition of religious experience. Nevertheless, Danto points to an important element in our use of expressions such as "mystical experience" and "religious experience". It would indeed be very curious if a person said that she had had a religious experience, but that this was a matter of no importance to her. And it would be even more curious if someone told us that she recently had a boring religious experience. We would be inclined to say that whatever experience she had, it was not a religious experience. We may conclude with the words of Vincent Brümmer: "In order to count as religious, an experience must be impressive or inspiring."[21]

5. When Swinburne describes the content of those experiences he wishes to call religious, he talks about those experiences *"which seem (epistemically) to the subject* to be an experience of God . . ."* (my italics). Here Swinburne relies upon a distinction made by Chisholm between the *epistemic* and the *comparative* uses of such verbs as 'seems', 'appears', 'looks', etc. To use such words in the epistemic sense is to describe what the subject is inclined to believe on the basis of his or her experience, and not (as in the comparative use) to compare the way an objects looks with the way it normally looks.

It is possible to avoid this problem altogether by restricting the field of religious experiences to *propositional religious experiences,* i.e. those experiences *which the subject judges to be* an experience of God etc. This description is—like Swinburne's—an internal description: it does not presuppose that the experience is veridical. But an internal description in terms of the judgement involved in the experience—and not in terms of what (epistemically) seems to be the case—makes clear that (1) the judgements involved are not necessarily arbitrary, i.e. the subject may have good reasons for judging his or her experience as an experience of God, and (2) that the judgement is a claim about how things really are, objectively. This is accurately emphazised by Vincent Brümmer. He concludes:

> In this way the believer claims that his interpretation of experience in the light of his faith represents things as they really are. In *interpreting* his experience, he recognizes what is really the case.[22]

In sum: internal descriptions of religious experience in terms of how the subject judges what he or she experiences are to be preferred before internal descriptions in terms of what (epistemically) seems to be the case.

6. Our next point is concerned with the content of the judgement which the subject having the experience is making in religious experiences. Swinburne speaks about such an experience "which seems (epistemically) to the subject to be *an experience of God (either of his just being there, or doing or bringing about something) or some other supernatural thing"*.[23] If the purpose of this definition of religious experiences "whose occurrence is supposed to be evi-

dence for the existence of God",[24] then I think it is too restricted. There are, I would argue, religious experiences which an experiencing subject would not judge as an experience of God or some other supernatural thing and which nevertheless could be supposed to be evidence for the existence of God, for example, experiences of transcendence. The concept of transcendence has fewer theological ramifications than the concept of God, i.e. experiences of transcendence could be used as evidence in contexts other than theism. But this does not imply that they are not of importance as evidence *also* within the context of theism.

What is meant by the expression "experience of transcendence"? Such an experience could be characterized as an experience which the experiencing subject judges to be an experience of a reality which transcends the physical world as well as the minds of human beings. Experiences of God could be regarded as determinates of a more general determinable experience of transcendence. Another determinate of the determinable experience of transcendence could be experiences of Brahman.[25]

7. Swinburne's definition is not only too restricted in that it includes only experiences which the subject judges to be experiences of God. It is also too wide in that it includes those experiences which involve a logical inference from what the person experiences to the properties of the object which the subject is judging. But we need some concept of religious experience which is distinct from the concept of religious belief. If we say that religious experiences are *ontologically direct,* then we would have a concept of religious experience which would be distinct from the concept of religious belief. But such a concept of religious experience would be far too narrow. It is better to make use of Mavrodes' concept of *psychological* immediacy. The term "religious experience" should be reserved for those mental phenomena, which display the quality of psychological immediacy (a quality which neither excludes nor implies that the experience is causally indirect).[26] The presence of reflective inference—and the absence of the quality of psychological immediacy—is the distinguishing mark of religious beliefs.

We may now sum up our seven points in this section and propose the following definition of religious experience. (Its aim is to describe those religious experiences whose occurrence could be supposed to be evidence for the existence of God.) An experience is a religious experience if it is an intentional experience which (a) has the quality of psychological immediacy, (b) the experiencing subject judges to be an experience of transcendence (or an experience which is a determinate of the determinable experience of transcendence) and (c) is impressive and inspiring.

This definition should be understood as a general *interal* description of a certain type of experience, which is considered as especially controversial from an epistemological point of view. Further, the definition includes only those religious experiences which are *intentional* and *propositional*. But it includes *both direct and indirect religious experiences*. And it is *not restricted to interpretative* religious experiences.

Classifying religious experience

Having decided the scope of an epistemologically relevant concept of religious experience, it is an interesting task to reflect upon the question how this field of religious experiences is to be differentiated. Different schemes of classification have been suggested by different scholars with apparently different purposes in mind. Ninian Smart, for example, makes an important distinction between mystical and numinous experiences. Numinous experiences are associated with worship and a personal conception of the supernatural. Mystical experiences are associated with meditation and an impersonal conception of reality.[27] William Wainwright supplements this scheme with a third class: ".... the experiences bound up with the devotional life of the ordinary believer (gratitude, love, trust, filial fear, etc)."[28] Peter Donovan proceeds from a scheme with four different classes: mystical, paranormal, charismatic and regenerative. He uses William James' analysis of mystical experiences to distinguish the first class; mystical experiences are ineffable, noetic, transient and passive. Paranormal experiences include experiences of parapsychological and spiritistic phenomena. Charismatic experiences—such as speaking in tungues and prophecying—form a third class, and conversion experiences (to which Donovan counts numinous experiences) form a fourth.[29]

These classifications proceed from considerations about the content of religious experiences. Other classifications have been suggested which are given from a more epistemological perspective. John J Shepard proposes the following distinction in his book *Experience, Inference and God*:

(1) experiences which stand or fall epistemologically either (*a*) with their own religious interpretation, or (*b*) with some other religious interpretation;
(2) experiences which do not so stand or fall.[30]

An experience of the Virgin might be an experience of type (1) (a). If the interpretation is false, then the person having the experience was subject to a vision devoid of any cognitive value. The veridicality of the experience is, in other words, wholly dependent upon the person's interpretation of the experience. But this is not the case with experience of the type (1) (b). A Sufi mystic may take an experience as an experience of union with Allah. And even if this interpretation is false, the experience might nevertheless be veridical if there exists some *other* religious interpretation of the experience which is true (for example the interpretation that the Sufi encountered the Zoroastrian god Ahura Mazda).

The most interesting type of religious experiences is, however, of type (2). Examples of such experiences are numinous experiences and experiences of contingency. These experiences can be veridical even if no religious interpretation of them is true. An atheist may accept his or her experience of the precariousness of existence, or have a sense of ontological shock at there being a world at all, as veridical. And he or she might share this conviction with a person, who provides these experiences with a religious interpretation (which may or may not be true). The veridicality of such experiences, is not dependant upon the truth of their religious interpretation—even if it is the case (as Shepard does not clearly observe) that if no religious interpretation of such experiences is true, then they cannot be veridical as experiences of a transcendent reality.[31]

A Swedish philosopher of religion, Ulf Hansson, has made an important effort to elucidate the notion of religious experience through linguistic and semantical analysis. Hansson claims that the expression "religious experience" sometimes occurs as a head term and sometimes as a normal expression. When the expression occurs as a head term the adjective and the substantive are joined together and it makes no sense to put the expression in the plural or add an undetermined article. But when the expression occurs as a normal expression the adjective functions as an independent qualifier of the substantive—and it is natural to put the expression in the plural or add an undetermined article. In this use it is natural to ask: what makes an experience religious? Hansson says that there may be three answers to this question. According to the *object analysis* what makes an experience religious is that it is an experience of something that is religious. According to the *adverbial analysis* it is an experience of something in a religious way. And according to the *subject analysis* it is an experience by a subject who is religious.[32]

This is not the place to evaluate the merits of these different schemes of classification. They are proposed with different purposes in mind. There appears to be many ways of structuring the phenomena brought together under the concept of religious experience. I shall conclude this section with some reflections which are raised by Ninian Smart's distinction between mystical and numinous experiences. First of all, I think it is clear that there are religious experiences which can be described as either mystical or numinous— even if there are border-line cases which are hard to classify. What is not entirely clear, however, is whether all mystical and numinous experiences can be called religious. There are, for example, some types of experiences, which can be described as experiences of unity with nature. Zaehner calls these experiences "panenhenic experiences".[33] The following short report—taken from an investigation by David Hay among post-graduate students—may serve as an example of such a type of experiences:

> It's like loosing your particular sense of identity and it's like, say, looking at a tree. You see certain things happening to the tree, and you have words to describe it. There's nothing between us, the tree and me.[34]

It is not uncommon that such an experience of unity with nature is regarded as a kind of mystical experience. But if we presuppose our earlier definition of religious experience (pp. 26 f.) then such a mystical experience cannot be called a religious experience—as far as it is possible to judge from such a short report. It contains no reference whatsoever to transcendence.

Similarly, it might be argued that even if the class of religious experiences contain numinous experiences, not all numinous experiences are religious. To be sure, Rudolf Otto would assert that numinous experiences involve an encounter with Deity. But Ronald Hepburn has argued that the essential qualities of awe and fascination in numinous experiences can be sensed without any conception of Deity. There is an analogue to—if not a form of—numinous experience in the aesthetic contemplation of nature, in which we are confronted with an overwhelming scene of beauty and majesty. No specific cognitive claims of being in the presence of Deity or a supernatural reality are associated with such acts of contemplation.[35] If this is correct, then there are numinous experiences which are not religious experiences.

As William Wainwright has argued, it is necessary to recognize that there are religious experiences, which are neither mystical nor numinous. Wainwright mentions the experiences of peace, bliss and love of the ordinary believer. Schleiermacher's idea of experiences of absolute dependence might also be mentioned in this context. The merits and limits of this idea are not always properly recognized. Schleiermacher's concept of experiences of absolute dependence must be seen against the background of a distinction between two states of consciousness: the state of reception and the state of action. When the subject is in a state or *reception,* then there is a *feeling of dependence.* On the other hand—when the subject is in a state of *action,* then there is a *feeling of freedom.* For many people life in the world appears as a series of feelings which are partly feelings of dependence, partly feelings of freedom. It may—says Schleiermacher—seem that a child's dependence upon his/her parents or a citizen's dependence upon powerful political authorities are pure and absolute. But even such situations of dependence always elicit some kind of counterreaction from the subject—accompanied by a feeling of freedom.

But there is a feeling of *absolute* dependence involving no activity of the subject. This feeling cannot be directed towards something delimited and finite, because then it would contain an element of counterreaction of the subject. Feelings of absolute dependence are directed—but not towards something delimited and finite. They are directed towards the infinite, which encompasses but goes beyond immediate self-consciousness.[36]

Schleiermacher's idea is suggestive, but it leaves certain problems unsolved.[37] It could be argued that the presence of the transcendent reality is not only experienced in conjunction with feelings of dependence but also in conjunction with feelings of freedom.[38] Another problem concerns the relationship between experiences of absolute dependence and the concept of God. How do we know that an experience of absolute dependence is also an experience of God? Says Schleiermacher:

> ... das Gottesbewusstsein [schliesst zugleich] so in das Selbstbewusstsein ein, dass beides ... nicht von einander getrennt werden kann. Das schlechthinnige Abhängigkeitsgefühl wird nur ein klares Selbstbewusstsein, indem zugleich diese Vorstellung wird.[39]

Schleiermacher seems to have been aware of the fact that it is not evident to everyone who has an experience of absolute dependence that this experience involves an experience of God. To be sure, serious reflection upon experiences of absolute dependence would reveal this to be a fact. But as long as *the subject does not take* the experience to have any evidential value for the existence or nature of God, an experience of absolute dependence cannot be taken as a religious experience. An experience of absolute dependence may, however, be transformed into a religious experience, if the person having the experience takes the experience as an experience of God (or some other supernatural reality) some time after the experience is over. Of course, such retrospective transformation in our understanding of earlier experiences is not restricted to experiences of absolute dependence. It may, however, be the case that there are distinctive types of experiences which are especially liable to a retrospective religious interpretation. Some types of nonreligious mystical and numinous experiences might belong to this category.[42] If this is the case, then this category of experiences would require the invention of a new concept; we might call them *semi-religious experiences*. They have the interesting property of, so to say, bridging the gap which is created by intensive conversions. They also have the property of being shared by both believers and non-believers. This is of a certain importance in the dialogue between believers and non-believers.

Some readers may feel inclined to direct a critique against the whole approach of the present chapter. They would argue that I have presupposed that it is possible to describe the religious experience. But this is to try to do something which cannot be done. It is impossible to conceptualize religious experiences. Therefore, they elude all pedestrian efforts to be defined or described. Religious experience is ineffable. The next chapter will be devoted to the problem raised by these objectors.

NOTES

[1] Hepburn 1967, p. 165.
[2] See for example, Hay 1982, part two.
[3] Mavrodes 1978, p. 236 f.
[4] Kierkegaard (Bind 6) 1963, pp. 135 f. and Heidegger 1953, pp. 184–191.
[5] Mavrodes 1978, p. 236.
[6] Chisholm 1966, pp. 10 f.
[7] See Marc-Wogau 1945, p. 27.—See also Oakes 1972, pp. 260 f.
[8] Marc-Wogau makes a similar distinction but uses a different terminology (Marc-Wogau 1945, pp. 29–31).—It must be observed that even if a judgement does not go beyond the content of the experience, it might nevertheless be the case that the content of the experience contains an clement which points beyond the experience. Many noninterpretative experiences are intentional experiences.
[9] Berkeley 1979, p. 32.
[10] Katz 1978.
[11] Hick 1966, p. 108.
[12] Hick 1966, pp. 114 f.
[13] Swinburne 1979, pp. 244 f.
[14] See further Mavrodes theory of input alignment in Mavrodes 1972, pp. 58 ff.
[15] George Mavrodes has underlined that it is possible to experience an object as well as infer it: "It will sometimes be the case that when the existence of properties of a certain entity 0 are being inferred from some other entity which is being experienced that it would be possible with the same input, to experience 0 instead." See Mavrodes 1972, p. 66.
[16] Hick argues that all religious experiences – including experiences of *unio mystica*—are in reality indirect. See Hick 1977, pp. 83 f.
[17] Swinburne 1979, p. 246.
[18] Sutherland 1977, p. 15.—See also Smart 1978, p. 20, Forell 1975, p. 85 and Smith 1968, pp. 36 f. and p. 55: "The proper interpretation of religion in terms of human experience coincides with the correct description, *not* of religious experience, but of the religious dimension of experience. Among the many dimensions or 'worlds' of meaning in which experience is taken and through which it is understood, stands the religious dimension, the dimension in which all is understood from the perspective of a worshipful being".
[19] Mavrodes 1978, pp. 235 f.
[20] Danto, 1976, p. 45.
[21] Brümmer 1979, p. 223.
[22] Brümmer 1984, p. 72.
[23] Swinburne 1979, p. 246. (My italics.)
[24] Swinburne 1979, p. 244.

[25] The concept of experiences of transcendence is less associated with the world-view of supranaturalism (see Tillich 1964, pp. 6 f.) than the concept of experiences of "some . . . supernatural thing". Therefore, I prefer the former concept.

[26] See above p. 72.

[27] Smart 1960, pp. 46–60 and 1972, pp. 24 f.

[28] Wainwright 1973, p. 257.

[29] See Donovan 1979, chapter 1.

[30] Shepard 1975, pp. 12 f.

[31] Shepard 1975, p. 13.

[32] See Hanson 1973, chapter 4.

[33] Zaehner 1957, pp. 28 f.

[34] Hay 1979, p. 179.

[35] Hepburn 1966, pp. 205 ff.—It is questionable if Hepburn would regard numinous experiences as intentional in the first place (see Hepburn 1966, p. 205).

[36] Schleiermacher 1927, p. 646.—See also Schleiermacher 1958, p. 32

[37] Jørgensen has an interesting discussion about Schleiermacher's later theory of religious experience. See Jørgensen 1977, pp. 214–246. See p. 214 note 5 for an extensive bibliography on the discussion about his famous idea of experiences of absolute dependence.

[38] See Pannenberg 1962, pp. 9 ff.

[39] Schleiermacher 1927, p. 648. See further Barth 1968.

[40] The following story (reported by Unger in Unger 1976, p. 158) is a good example or a retrospective transformation of a person's understanding of an earlier experience:

During spring 1929 (when I was almost 11), I was hopping from ice-floe to ice-floe on the Ume River and happened to get caught between some floes. One of my friends who was also there grabbed my hand and held me up while we drifted down the river towards the lumber-receiving station at Öhn, a few miles downriver. He prayed and I prayed and everything turned out so luckily that we were rescued. I had to be taken to Umeå Hospital, where after a few days I caught pneumonia. *While drifting in the icecold water I experienced something which I later was able to identify as God's saving hand.* Of relevance here is the fact that my mother (since deceased) had a sort of vision of my troubled situation and, without knowing the true situation, prayed to God to save me from danger.

After Confirmation I have regularly attended church with thanksgiving and prayed, but have never again reexperienced the confrontation which I had while still young.

Chapter 2

The conceptualization of religious experience

In his well-known book *He Who Is*, Eric Mascall considers religious experience as a possible ground for belief in God. He concludes that while by no means without all value from a cognitive point of view, religious experience possesses "the disadvantage, from an apologetic point of view, that, while it may be completely convincing to those who have it, it is incommunicable to those who have not."[1]

If Mascall is correct then the value of religious experience in Christian theology would be considerably diminished. Mascall accepts the essential content of religious experience as characterized by Rudolf Otto in his famous book *The Idea of the Holy*. Other thinkers—such as Walter Stace—have emphasized the incommunicable character of *mystical* experiences. Needless to say, it might be argued that there are religious experiences which are neither numinous nor mystical but communicable. This may be the case. But if numinous and mystical experiences are impossible to communicate to those who have not had them, this must have decisive consequences for the work of the Christian theologian.

The purpose of this chapter is to analyze some arguments for the claim that certain important forms of religious experiences are incommunicable or ineffable. It is important to distinguish between two versions of this claim. In a strong version of the claim, it is denied that any concept, present, past or future, is applicable to the object of the religious experience in question. The object of religious experiences is ineffable *in principle*. A weaker version of the claim is that the object of the experience cannot be described with the help of any concepts which are at our disposal in the present situation. According to the weaker version, the object of religious experiences is ineffable *in practice*.[2]

The claim that the object of *mystical* experiences is in principle ineffable, has been very influential in the Christian church ever since its beginnings. The arguments for this claim have, however, varied considerably. One kind of argument departs from the character of the mystical experience *itself*. Other arguments presuppose a certain preconceived doctrine about the *object* of mystical experiences. Still other arguments involve considerations about the *subject* of mystical experiences. We shall look at some examples of these different kinds of reasonings. Let us first, however, consider an argument from the character of numinous experiences.

Ineffability and the character of numinous experiences

Rudolf Otto introduced the concept of numinous feeling, which has been very influential since it appeared in his book *Das Heilige* (first published 1917). Numinous feelings are the human response to an encounter with a mysterious object. These feelings are feelings of awe and wonder, but also fascination. Otto detects traces of such experiences—or aspects of such experiences—in primitive and crude feelings of uncanniness, of being possessed by demons, of ghosts and haunted places. In the established religions we find more balanced and developed expressions of such experiences in experiences of God and mystical experiences. One example is, of course, Isaiah's vision in the temple.

Otto makes many claims about these experiences and what finally emerges, is a general theory of religion. Here we shall focus on his claim that the numinous object is in principle ineffable. Says Otto:

> Er bleibt in unauflöslichen Dunkel des rein Gefühlsmässigen, unbegrifflichen Erfahrens. Und nur durch die Notenschrift der deutenden Ideogramme ist er andeutbar. Das heisst für uns: er ist irrational.[3]

With many examples from different religious traditions, Otto tries to make it credible that there is a distinctive kind of experience which displays this quality of being in principle ineffable. It is certainly an impressive picture, which Otto gives us. His phenomenological approach is a stimulating counterweight to other more rationalistic approaches to religious experience.

But that which is Otto's strength is at the same time his weakness. We may ask: how is it possible to arrive at the conclusion that the numinous object is *in principle* ineffable on the basis of a phenomenological survey of different testimonies of religious experiences? The frequency of pious men and women claiming that the object is in principle ineffable, cannot be a sufficient reason for the reflective theologian to assert that the numinous object is indeed in principle ineffable. The bold and controversial thesis that there are no concepts, and there will never be any concepts, which are applicable to the numinous object, must be defended by stronger arguments than the conviction of many pious men and women. But as far as I can see no such supplementary argument occurs in Otto's influential book.

Ineffability and the character of mystical experiences

There is one other argument which might be taken as an argument from the *quality* of *mystical* experiences. It is found in the writings of Plotinos and quoted by Walter Stace. Stace cites the following passage from Plotinos' greatest work, *The Enneads*:

No doubt we should not speak of seeing but, instead of seen and seer, speak boldly of a simple unity. For in this seeing we neither distinguish nor are there two. The man . . . is merged with the Supreme, one with it. Only in separation is there duality. *This is why the vision baffles telling; for how can a man bring back tidings of the Supreme as detached* when he has seen it as one with himself . . .[4]

Stace claims that Plotinos has detected a basic and inherent *logical* reason for—and not merely and *emotional cause of*—the claim that it is impossible to apply concepts to the object of mystical experience.

To describe something implies that it stands over against one as an object to be looked at and examined and have its characteristics noted. But this condition of description is not fulfilled in the experience of the One, since the experiencer is merged in it, one with it, and without any separation from it.[5]

I must admit that I fail to see in what way the conclusion that mystical experiences are in principle ineffable follows from the premise that in the mystical experience "the man . . . is merged with the Supreme, one with it". Many human beings have had the experience of being totally absorbed by an interest or a feeling. In fact, many feelings encompass our whole being. And it seems to be true that if we try to make deep anger or deep joy the object of reflection, then we are no longer in the same state of consciousness as we were, before the idea of such a reflection upon our state of consciousness occurred. But from the fact that we cannot perform an act of reflection at the same time as we are in a state of deep emotion, it does not follow that an act of reflection is impossible. Surely, such an act of reflection (involving the application of concepts) is possible after the emotional experience has faded away. It is retained in memory and we might reflect upon its causes, qualities and effects. Why should it be impossible to perform a similar kind of reflection after mystical experiences? The fact that our whole being is submerged in an experience of total unity, cannot make an act of reflection after the experience is over, impossible.

In fact, Stace admits that such acts of reflection and application of concepts to the experience are possible. Stace claims that the basic reason for the mystics to claim that their experience is ineffable does not lie in the fact that they find it impossible to describe the object of their experience. However, they find it impossible to describe *without lapsing into logical contradictions.*[6] This theory is not very credible; many mystics claim that their experiences are ineffable before or without having made serious efforts to arrive at a non-contradictory account of their experiences.

Religious experiences touch the innermost springs of a person's life and decisions. But the reflective activity of finding an adequate description of such experiences presupposes an attitude of detachment. Plotinos' claim that there is total unity between subject and object and this is why "the vision baffles telling" need not be interpreted as a logical reason for ineffability in principle. It may be interpreted as an expression of embarrassment when urged to take an attitude of an observer towards an experience in which he found himself deeply and personally involved. Such an embarressment is also expressed in the following quotation from Dag Hammarskjöld's book *Markings*:

> There is a pride of faith, more unforgivable and dangerous than any pride of the intellect. It reveals a split personality in which faith is 'observed' and appraised, thus negating the unity born of a dying-unto-self, which is the definition of faith.[7]

Ineffability and the object of mystical experiences

The claim that the object of mystical experiences is in principle ineffable, can also be based on a certain preconceived doctrine about the nature of this object. Neoplatonism is one example of a doctrine, which has provided an important framework for the interpretation of mystical experience as ineffable in principle and has strongly underlined the transcendence and inscrutability of the object of mystical experience, the One.[8] The foundation for this is the claim that the object of mystical experience is the absolute simplicity of the One. Concepts are designed for the discernment of differences. Therefore, the experience of the One *must* be beyond *all* concepts. Through the writings ascribed to Dionysios Areopagita (presumably, a Christian theologian from the 6th century A.D.) this neoplatonistic doctrine has exercised influence upon theological tradition in the East as well as in the West. It is a matter of controversy how deep the details of *Plotinos'* doctrine have penetrated the thought of Pseudo Dionysios. But it appears more or less clear that he derives his claim for the ineffability of the object of mystical experience from a doctrine about the object of mystical experiences which is not identical with Plotinos' doctrine. Lossky claims that whereas Plotinos affirms that the One is simple, Pseudo Dionysios claims that God even transcends the difference between simplicity and multiplicity. God is incomprehensible *by nature*.[9] This comes to the foreground in the following quotation by Vladimir Lossky:

> ... he [i.e. Pseudo Dionysios] makes it ... clear that even though we attain to the highest peaks accessible to created beings, the only rational notion which we can have of God will still be that of His imcomprehensibility. Consequently, theology must be not so much a quest of positive notions about the divine being as an experience which surpasses all understanding.[11]

A different doctrine about the object of mystical experiences is found in Henri Bergson's influential book *The Two Sources of Morality and Religion*. An essential part of this doctrine is the claim that the object of mystical experiences is in principle ineffable, but Bergson's doctrine about the nature of the object of mystical experiences (which is the foundation for the claim that it is in principle ineffable) has a highly original content. Bergson departs from a dualistic ontology, which includes two fundamental principles or aspects: there is in reality a creative, living and dynamic element which is opposed to another reproductive, material and static element. The creative element is in *Two Sources* described as a vital impetus (it is unclear how this concept if related to earlier descriptions of the dynamic element, e.g. "la dureé réelle", "évolution créatrice".[11]) Life is a manifestation of this vital impetus. And life can be described as a creative effort to transcend external material conditions—and not passively adapt to them—, to overcome resistance and obstacles and to develop into more complex forms. This creative effort cannot be explained with reference to physics or chemistry; it requires the introduction of new concept: the vital impetus, which cannot be reduced to physical and chemical concepts. It is of course an interesting question whether the creative efforts displayed in biological evolution can be explained without the introduction of a new ontological category: the vital impetus. But this is not the important question in the present context. What is important, is his interpretation of mystical experience.

Bergson's dualistic ontology is associated with a dualistic epistemology. There are two ways of knowing: intellect and intuition. These ways of knowing correspond to the two elements of reality in his ontology. The vital impetus of "real duration" cannot be grasped with the intellect. It is in principle beyond all concepts. Concepts are designed to freeze and isolate—and thereby distort—our intuition of a reality in constant dynamic and creative development.[12]

Mystical experience is, now, interpreted as an intense intuition of the vital impetus. Bergson says:

> In our eyes, the ultimate end of mysticism is the establishment of a contact, consequently of a partial coincidence, with the creative effort which life itself manifests. This effort is of God, if it is not God himself. The great mystic is to be conceived as an individual being, capable on transcending the limitations imposed on the species by its material nature, thus continuing and extending the divine action.[13]

An important question concerns the concept of God presupposed in the quotation. If God is identified with the vital impetus, then God is not infinite as

Christian theology has affirmed, because the material environment is an *obstacle* for his self-fulfilment and actualization.

It is through his doctrine of the vital impetus that Bergson expounds his interpretation of mystical experience. His doctrine of the vital impetus also enables him to make a distinction between dynamic and static religion; the dynamic religion of experience and the static religion of dogma (this distinction bears resemblance to similar distinctions by James).[14] But the controversial character of this doctrine makes the value of this theory of religious experience uncertain.[15]

Before leaving this kind of defence for the thesis that the object of mystical experience is in principle ineffable, the following question must be asked: is it not a clear contradiction involved in the effort to defend the claim that the object of mystical experience is in principle ineffable with reference to a doctrine about the nature of this object? A doctrine about the nature of the object of mystical experiences would seem to involve some positive notion of this object. But the possibility of forming such positive notions is clearly denied by those who claim that the mystical object is in principle ineffable.

It seems very difficult to escape this objection to the proposed line of argument. We may claim that the mystical object is simple (as Plotinos) and therefore in principle ineffable, because concepts always differentiate. Or we may claim that the mystical object is dynamic (as Bergson) and therefore in principle ineffable, because concepts are static. Some positive notion about the mystical objects still forms the point of departure. So the ineffability-thesis must be qualified accordingly. What can be argued is only a *partial* ineffability in principle, i.e. ineffability with regard to all concepts *except* the concept of simplicity, vital impetus etc.

With respect to Pseudo Dionysios' thesis that there is only *one* concept applicable to God, i.e. his incomprehensiblity, things stand a little different as has been shown by W.E. Kennick. If a theologian claims that "God is in principle ineffable", this may be considered as clearly contradictory, because something is said about God, namely that God is in principle ineffable. But—as Kennick has pointed out—the claim that God is in principle ineffable can be interpreted as a metalinguistic statement, which can be formulated in the following way: for all sentences about God it holds that they express no fact about God.

But even if it is possible to argue in this way, it is very likely that a contradiction occurs when it comes to the question: why would some sentences about God form the content of a theology and not other? It seems difficult to imagine a criterion which does not—implicitly or explicitly—make some reference to the actual nature of the mystical object. Pseudo Dionysios finds such a criterion in divine revelation.[16] Such a reference presupposes a claim that God is such as God has revealed God's self. But this is a positive claim about the mystical object and as such it would contradict the claim that the mystical object is in principle ineffable.

Ineffability and the subject of mystical experiences

A third kind of argument for the claim that the object of mystical experiences is in principle ineffable, involves considerations about the subject of these experiences, e.g. the nature of human beings. It would seem possible to debart from a doctrine about the limits of human understanding. The philosophy of Kant contains such a doctrine about the absolute limits of human thought. We can apprehend phenomena, but not what lies beyond these phenomena. The young Wittgenstein developed a doctrine in *Tractatus* that human understanding is delimited by the structure of human language. Wittgenstein concluded: "What we cannot speak about we must pass over in silence."[17] We shall not digress into an analysis of these controversial theories about the absolute limits of human understanding.[18] It is not impossible that a defence of the ineffability of the object of mystical experiences, can be found along this line of thought. There is an argument in a recent book by Peter Donovan, which can be seen in this perspective. According to Donovan:

> ... it is characteristic of mystical and religious thinking to believe that what is encountered in religious experience, God or absolute reality, Brahman or the Void, is *ultimate. Human thought which is nonultimate, cannot set bounds to an ultimate reality.* No concepts can be finally applied to it, since the possiblity that they will need revising and replacing remains permently open. Therefore all that is said is said provisionally, and is at best only partially the truth of the matter. The traditional Christian term for this idea has been the doctrine of God's *incomprehensibility.*[19]

Donovan's point is *not* that it is impossible to apply some kind of concept upon that which is encountered in the religious experience. His point is rather that no concept can be applied without acknowledging that the possiblity for its revision or replacement remains permanently open. It is—in other words—impossible to say that a certain concept once and for all applies to the object of, say, mystical or numinous experiences. "Human thought which is nonultimate, cannot set bounds to an ultimate reality".

Donovan's idea of the impossibility of ultimately applying any concept to that which is encountered at least in some important forms of religious experiences, has the merit that it does justice to the perplexing character of those experiences without denying the possibility of some kind of talk about what is encountered. Says Donovan:

When it is said that God (or some other ultimate reality) is inexpressible, this must be taken to mean not that one can say absolutely nothing about God, but rather that one can say nothing *absolutely* about God. For God would not be an ultimate reality if any words or descriptions could fully comprehend or be "the last word" on the subject.[20]

A final remark about myths, metaphors and analogies

Before we leave the question about the ineffability of mystical experiences, we must make one important remark. It is one thing to say that the object of mystical or other religious experiences is in principle ineffable. It is quite another thing to assert that the object of certain religious experiences cannot be understood through the use of certain methods of analysis, for example the methods of analysis used in rational disciplines such as natural science. It seems quite reasonable to affirm that the object of certain religious experiences cannot be described with scientific concepts with the demands of precision and consistency these concepts are subject to. But this is not the same thing as to claim that these religious experiences are in principle ineffable. The *way* we describe and explain objects and events within the sciences, is certainly different from the way we describe and explain the (alleged) object of religious experiences. Adequate communication of religious experiences requires the use of myths, metaphors, and analogies. This should not be interpreted as meaning that the way we describe and explain objects in science is *fundamentally* different from the way this is done in religion. Such a claim presupposes that there exists some kind of watertight bulkhead between scientific and religious understanding. There are certainly differences, but there are also some interesting analogies, which Ian Barbour has focused upon in his highly interesting book *Myth, Models and Paradigms* (Barbour 1974).

In this chapter I have argued that even if there is a sense in which we may say that no concepts are wholly adequate for the object of religious experiences, it is nevertheless unjustified to claim that the object or religious experiences is beyond conceptualization. But—we may say—it is one thing to argue that the object of religious experience can be conceptualized. It is quite another thing to argue that a certain conceptualization of religious experience is possible. One of the most influential ways in which religious experience has been conceptualized is the theistic one. In theistic religions, believers often judge their religious experiences as experiences of God. But is it really possible to describe a religious experience in such a way? This question will be examined in the next chapter.

NOTES

[1] Mascall 1958, p. 29.
[2] This distinction is inspired by W.E. Kennick's article on the ineffable in *Encyclopedia of Philosophy* (Kennick 1967, p. 181).—As Kennick underlines the ineffable must not be confused with the unknowable. It is possible to know something, even if we find it impossible to put it into words.
[3] Otto 1925, p. 70.
[4] Stace 1960, p. 104. (My italics.)
[5] Stace 1960, p. 105
[6] Stace 1960, pp. 304 ff.
[7] Hammarskjöld 1980, p. 97.
[8] For a more detailed analysis concerning the relationship between Plato and Plotinos, see Ivanka 1964, pp. 70 ff. and 77 ff.
[9] See Lossky 1957, pp. 29 ff. and Ivanka 1964, pp. 262–289. See also Dionysios 1975, pp. 142 f.
[10] Lossky 1957, p. 38. It is not evident that this is a correct interpretation of Pseudo Dionysios' position. According to one of his most well-known books—*On Divine Names*—ultimate reality involves a rational as well as an irrational aspect. See Ivanka 1964, p. 258.
[11] Goudge 1967, p. 294.
[12] See Bergson 1935, pp. 334 f.
[13] Bergson 1935, pp. 220 f.
[14] See James 1974, pp. 48 ff.
[15] For a more detailed analysis of Bergson's theory of religion, see Moore 1938 and Sundén 1940.
[16] Dionysios 1975, p. 55.
[17] Wittgenstein 1969, p. 151.
[18] For a discussion about this aspect of the philosophy of Kant and Wittgenstein, see Pears 1971, pp. 11–41.
[19] Donovan 1979, p. 33 (my italics). See also Hudson 1974, pp. 23 ff. on the concept of *open-texture*.
[20] ibid.

Chapter 3

Are experiences of God possible?

The question in the title of this chapter may seem peculiar to some people. We may doubt the existence of God. But to doubt the existence of experiences that could be described as experiences of God seems to be doubting something which is before our very eyes. Recently, a collegue of mine published a book about experiences of God.[1] It is introduced with six reports about intensive experiences of God. And holy scriptures and different religious traditions supply us with ample material on the subject.

Yet there is still room for some kind of doubt. The Jewish-Christian tradition has always been somewhat embarrassed when it comes to experiences of God. According to Exodus 33:20, the Lord tells Moses that "you cannot see my face; for man shall not see me and live." And John in his first letter tells us that "no man has ever seen God . . ." (4:12). These words could, possibly, be taken as expressions of the fear within the Jewish and Christian religion of anthropomorphism. This reluctance to speak of experiences of God is also clear in the following quotation from an article by H.H. Price. It comes from a discussion about the possibility to know God not only by description but also by acquaintance:

> The claim to *know* the One and Only Lord of All is so enormous that one shudders at it. Perhaps it might be just allowable to use the word 'aquaintance' by itself, omitting the phrase 'knowledge by'. We might, perhaps, say that we have come to be acquainted with God—just a very, very little—whereas before, at the most, we had only believed propositions about him. But even this language seems to me somewhat presumptuous.[2]

The concept of experiences of God is—in other words—very doubtful from a religious point of view. But critical questions concerning this concept can also be raised from a philosophical point of view. Does God have such attributes— according to the Jewish-Christian tradition—that it is possible to speak of an experience of God? In other words: does the proposition "A experiences (has an experience of) x" have implications which contradicts the proposition "x is God"? If this is the case, then one is justified in saying that there is no intelligible concept for an experience of God, because the (alleged) concept of an experience of God is an example of a *contradictio in adiecto,* i.e. one attributes a predicate to a concept which is incompatible with it. Experience of

God is impossible in the same sense as a square circle is impossible. This means the same thing as the claim that experiences of God (and sqaure circles) are *logically* impossible.

Thus, we can formulate the following three questions:

(1) are experiences of God logically possible?
(2) are there any experiences of God?
(3) are experiences of God experiences of something real?

I would argue that these three questions must be separated from each other. It is possible to answer the first question in the positive and yet answer question (2) and (3) in the negative. But if (1) is answered in the negative, then it is superfluous to discuss answers to question (2) and (3).

In this chapter I shall concentrate on question (1). (Questions (2) and (3) will be discussed in chapter 6–10). I shall discuss five arguments for the claim that question (1) should be answered in the negative. And I shall argue that all of these arguments are—for one reason or another—untenable.

Experiences of God and the existence of God

Some would argue that it is impossible to experience God, because God does not exist. This argument could be reconstructed in the form of the following inference:

(1) "*A* experiences (has an experience of) *x*" implies that "*x* exists"
(2) God does not exist
(3) It is not the case that *A* experiences (has an experience of) God

This argument is obviously defective. In the first premise (1) it is presupposed that "*A* experiences (has an experience of) *x*" is an external description of an experience. But "*A* experiences (has an experience of) *x*" can be understood as an equivalent of the *internal* description "*A* judges his or her experience to be an experience of *x*". But such an internal description of an experience does *not* imply the existence of the intentional object of the experience.[2]

Secondly, it could be argued that premise (2) is untenable, because there exists no conclusive evidence to the effect that the existence of God must be denied. This argument against (2) is, I think, correct. But because premise (1) is obviously false, there is no need to enter into a lengthy discussion about premise (2). If (1) is false, (3) does not follow even if (2) is true.

In the remaining part of this chapter "*A* experiences (has an experience of) *x*" should be understood as an *internal* description of an experience.

But there are other people who would say that it is impossible to experience God because God is infinite. Arguments of this type can be found in the writings of Ronald Hepburn[3] and—more clearly—of John Hick.[4] The following quotation from Hick concerns the impossibility of recognizing an infinite Being. But in connection with this Hick gives an argument against specific experiences of God:

> One can recognize that a being whom one encounters has a given finite degree of power, but how does one recognize that he has unlimited power? How does one perceive that his goodness and love, although appearing to exceed any human goodness and love, are actually infinite? Such qualities cannot be given in human experience. One might claim to have encountered a Being whom one presumes, or trusts, or hopes to be God; but one cannot claim to have encountered a Being whom one *recognized* to be the infinite, almighty, eternal Creator.[5]

Hick's argument can be comprehended in the following way:

(1) "*A* experiences (has an experience of) *x*" implies that "*x* is finite."
(2) God is infinite.
(3) It is not the case that *A* experiences (has an experience of) God.

To be clear about this argument we must make a distinction between the *mathematical* concept of infinity and the *mystical* concept of infinity.

The mathematical concept of infinity is presupposed in certain descriptions of space, time and number series. We say that space or time is infinite, or that the set of real numbers is infinite. We mean—to put it crudely—that there are no limits to space or time or the set of real numbers. Similarly, it is claimed that God is infinite, i.e. there are no limits to his power, knowledge, goodness etc. (This does not mean that God could not limit God's self, e.g. not exercise all of God's power.[6])

Then there is the mystical concept of infinity. Walter Stace calls this concept "the religious infinite" and explains it in the following way:

> The religious infinite, or in other words the infinity of God, means *that than which there is no other*. In this sense neither space nor time could be infinite, since space is an "other" to time, and time is an "other" to space.
> – – –
>
> It is evident that the infinity of God is no more than another name for His Oneness. And this Oneness is not the idea of the mathematical unit. It is the idea that neither within God nor outside Him is there any otherness, any division, any relation—for though we speak of the relation of God to the world, this, as we shall see, is a metaphor.[7]

Given this distinction, we may formulate the following two questions:

(1) is it logically possible for a person to experience the limitlessness of God's power, goodness, knowledge etc.?
(2) is it logically possible for a person to experience the Oneness of God?

Hick gives a negative answer to the first question. Human persons cannot experience the limitlessness of God, because they are finite creatures. Lawrence Becker has made an interesting comment to this negative answer. He argues that a distinction must be made between *encountering in toto an infinity* of something and *knowing that what you encounter is infinite*. It is, surely, impossible for finite creatures to encounter infinity in toto, let alone the infinity of God.

But this does not imply that it is impossible to know that whay you encounter is infinite. Says Becker:

> Take a familiar analog from mathematics: there are perfectly respectable ways of proving a collection infinite without demanding experience of the totality: e.g. the set of real numbers. To fail to see how a proof of equal stature is possible for 'unlimited power' is to exhibit a decided lack of imagination. One could get such a proof in the event that he understood a *principle* ('by which' the power 'operated') which entailed the conclusion that the power was unlimited.[8]

Or to take another example: looking at the starry heaven a cloudless winter-night I may sense the boundlessness of the universe. How is this sense of infinity to be described? Needless to say, I do not encounter the boundlessness of the universe *in toto*. Still it might be said that I experience the boundless universe *because I know that what I experience is boundless*. And this piece of knowledge is based upon certain elementary knowledge of astronomy and the theory of relativity. Similarly, it is logically possible to experience an infinite Being; not, of course, in the sense of experiencing this Being in toto, but in the sense of experiencing—or glancing—a Being whose properties we know are without limits. There are of course considerable problems in showing that such knowledge exists. But this is another matter.

Our second question concerned the logical possibility of a person experiencing the Oneness of God. Walter Stace claims that it is impossible to experience the Oneness of God with the help of concepts. The Oneness of God implies that God is without otherness, division or relation; but such a Being cannot be apprehended with concept "because the very nature of the concept is to work through otherness, division, and relation."[9] But—says Stace—the Oneness, or Infinity of God can be apprehended in religious intuition. The human mind does not only work with the help of concepts; it may encounter reality in a direct intuition.

This solution of the problem rests upon a particular view of the capacities of the human mind. More specifically, Stace presupposes that to have and use a concept is equivalent to separate and make distinctions. But to have and work with a concept might also involve such acts as unifying, synthezising and comprehending. If the intellectual function of concepts is looked upon in this perspective, then the problem of experiencing the Oneness of God disappears without presupposing a special religious faculty of the human mind.

In sum: premise (1) of the argument on p. 44 is not necessarily true. And—we might add—some qualification is also necessary as regards the second premise (2). Some theologians have argued that—for example— God's power is infinite in principle but not in fact. In fact it is limited by the freedom of human beings—and, possibly, by the freedom of other finite beings. In other words: everything that happens, does not happen because of God's will.

Can immanence capture transcendence?

Some thinkers would say that the transcendence of God makes it impossible to experience God. This argument can be elaborated in the form of the following inference

(1) "A experiences (has an experience of) x" implies that "x is immanent."
(2) God is transcendent.
(3) It is not the case that A experiences (has an experience of) God.

This argument (and particularly premise (1)) cannot be understood unless the concept of transcendence is made more precise.

It is not uncommon to describe experiences of transcendence in *epistemological* terms: experiences of transcendence are experiences of something "beyond the senses". If experiences of God are understood as experiences of something "beyond the senses", then (perhaps) a necessary element of experiences of God is underlined; but experiencing something "beyond the senses" is not necessarily experiencing God. Hampus Lyttkens has noted that "if a parapsychological experience like telepathy is made probable we have an example of an experience that is beyond our senses and still immanent".[10] If Lyttkens is correct—and I think he is—then parapsychologists and theologians are equally challenged by the question of the logical possibility of experiences of things "beyond the senses". Needless to say, this challenge could easily be evaded by postulating religious or other unknown psychic capacities of the human mind besides the senses. But if we deny ourselves this loophole, is there any other possibility of defending the logical coherence of speaking about "experiences of things 'beyond the senses'"? Focusing upon the problem of experiencing God, Robert Oakes has formulated the problem in the following way: it is logically possible for there to occur sensory detections of the presence of a being who is essentially unobservable? With the help of an ingenious example, Oakes claims that "Necessarily, God is unobservable" does *not* entail "Necessarily, God is such that there never occur cases in which his presence is detected by the senses".[11] And if this is the case, then it is logically possible that God may be detected through the senses, even if it is the case that God is essentially unobservable. The central argument for this is that unobservable entitites may have effects which are sensorily detectable. More specifically, it is possible for finite creature to "become aware of *God's* presence *in the very act of* perceiving the setting sun (or some other natural object/event) and thus to have sensory detections of (hence perceptual knowledge of) God's presence."[12] And it should be added: even if God is essentially unobservable. I think that Oakes has shown that it is logically possible to speak of experiences of a God who exists "beyond the senses"—without presupposing that the human mind has extraordinary cognitive capacities besides the senses and the intellect.

Some thinkers have searched for a uniquely religious concept of transcendence, i.e. a sense of the word which could be uniquely ascribed to God and to no other thing. It has been suggested that God is transcendent not only in the sense that God is "beyond the senses", but also in the sense that God is "beyond space and time". If the problem with the former concept is that it is too broad (it also covers parapsychological experiences), the problem with this idea of transcendence as "beyond space and time" is that it might be too narrow (is it necessarily the case that God is "beyond space and time?"[13]). But we shall not go into these problems in the present context. Let us instead focus upon the central problem in this section: is it logically possible to speak of experiences of things "beyond space and time"? Hampus Lyttkens answers this question in the negative:

> It is not possible in principle for one man living in immanence to *experience* something beyond time and space. Finitum non capax infiniti! What comes to us as experience with objective reference, is confined to a world in space and time.[13a]

Lyttkens does not give us any substantial argument for his claim that it is logically incoherent to speak of "experiences of transcendence" (in the sense of experiences of things "beyond space and time"). He seems to find this self-evident. I would argue that this may be so from a particular philosophical position. But there are elements within this philosophical position which could incline us towards another answer—and, more significantly, ther are alternative philosophical positions which clearly do not imply that it is incoherent to speak of experiences of transcendence.

The philosophy of Immanuel Kant provides a philosophical startingpoint from which it might be argued that experiences of things "beyond space and time" are in principle impossible. Kant argued that space and time should be regarded as forms of intuition. Space and time are not qualities of objective reality; they are, rather, formative principles of the human mind. They mould our sensual impressions into sense-perceptions. And since these principles are permanent qualities of the cognitive capacity of man, nothing can be apprehended unless it bears the stamp of these formative principles. Similarly, our thinking is affected by the influence of other forms of principles; basic concepts such as cause and effect and other "categories of human understanding" are inescapable features of the way we as humans conceive reality.

From this perspective it is impossible to speak of experiences of things "beyond space and time". Everything is apprehended according to these forms of intuition and human beings cannot escape this limitation of their sensual "systems".

There are, however, certain developments of this basic philosophical position inspired by efforts to accomodate the concept of transcendence. There are thinkers (such as Rudolf Otto and Anders Nygren) who have suggested that there exists a specific religious category. Anders Jeffner has drawn attention to the fact that Paul Tillich—arguing from a Kantian point of view—claims that there is a special religious kind of knowledge without introducing a special religious category. There is—says Tillich—a transcendental dimension in every cognitive act, because in every cognitive act we can become aware that reality is much greater than the part of it we succeed in capturing in our system of categories (and forms of inutition). Religious knowledge is based upon such an experience of transcendence.[14] Something similar has been argued by Ian Ramsey in his famous book on religious language. Ramsey says that there are certain situations in which we experience the world as "spatio-temporal and more". He continues:

> Without such 'depth'; without this which is 'unseen', no religion will be possible; though of course for a developed theology much else needs to be said. But here is the bridge-head, the base, call it what we will.[15]

Hence, it seems possible to preserve a Kantian outlook and, yet, argue that experiences of things "beyond space and time" are logically possible in a particular sense of the expression.

Needless to say, the logical possibility of experiencing things "beyond space and time" could also be defended if there is reason to assume that Kant's basic assumptions concerning space and time are incorrect. Suppose—contrary to

Kant—that space and time are objective features of the empirical world, and *not* structures in our cognitive ability. As long as humans direct their attention to the empirical world, the spatial and temporal qualities of this world will be reflected in their experiences. But it does not seem in principle impossible for human beings to direct their attention to things beyond the empirical world, eventually to a dimension of reality "beyond space and time" (if there is such a reality). If they did, we could perhaps expect that their spatio-temporal "habits" would linger on. Psychologically it could be difficult for them to free themselves from the modes of thinking appropriate in the empirical world, but inadequate when it comes to the intuition of the world "beyond". But if we start from a viewpoint other than the Kantian one, I see no reason why we should assume that experiences of things "beyond space and time" are in principle impossible.

Needless to say, there is another problem in this context which cannot be bypassed. It might be argued that experiences of things "beyond space and time" are not in principle impossible; but they are not as common as we think and—more specifically—they are not at all as frequent in the Bible as some of us would expect. This is an important point in the already quoted essay by Lyttkens. He asks us to consider some examples. Consider the story of Isaiah's experience in Isaiah 6. Lyttkens claims that the idea of transcendence (in the sense of "beyond space and time") "belongs to a level other than the vision itself; it belongs to the level of interpretation. And the reason for that must be found elsewhere, not in the vision itself."[16]

It is somewhat unclear, what is meant by the phrase "the vision *itself*" (my italics). Lyttkens passes easily from the story to the real event. This is, of course very dangerous, but let us pass over this problem. Lyttkens seems to be quite correct in his observation that the idea of transcendence (in the sense "beyond space and time") is not explicitly present in the testimony of Isaiah's vision. But one might still ask if there are not clearly discernible *clues* to transcendence in the story. One seraphim calls the other and says: "Holy, holy, holy is the Lord of hosts; the whole earth is full of his glory" (Is 6:3). The holiness of Jahve permeates the whole vision. And, most significantly, fundamental to the idea of holiness is "that of *otherness* or *separation,* of something *marked off* or *set apart.*" In the words of W.D. Hudson:

. . . it is not inappropriate to regard the concept of divine transcendence as the form which the idea of the otherness of the holy has assumed within theism.[17]

We must grant Lyttkens the point that the narrative of Isaiah's vision does not contain clear ideas of an experience "beyond space and time". Nevertheless, it might be argued that the idea of such an experience can be seen as an attempt to express a central *quality* of the vision as it is brought to us by the words in the book of Isaiah namely that of *divine otherness*. In other words: the story in Isaiah 6 contains certain clues to a concept of Deity, which is transcendent in the sense of "beyond space and time". Needless to say, such a concept of Deity may have other sources than an experience of holiness, e.g. a theory of transcendence. But it is questionable whether this in itself justifies Lyttkens' affirmation that the idea of transcendence does not belong to the level of the vision "itself" but to the level of "interpretation". The distinction between "the vision itself" and "the interpretation of the vision" is indeed important, but it easily blinds us to the fact that there are important relationships between the two. Lyttkens' analysis is captured by the analogy between religious experience and sense experience. But—as Vincent Brümmer has argued in a reply to Lyttkens' paper—this might in certain situations be a misleading analogy.[18]

God and the causes of religious experiences

It could further be argued that it is impossible to experience God, because it is impossible that God can be the *cause* of an experience.

This argument proceeds from an influential conception of human experience, which has its roots in the empiricism of John Locke. It is sometimes called the causal theory of perception. The main idea is that perception (and more broadly, experience) must be analyzed in terms of what causes the perception or experience. We shall not enter into a detailed analysis of this theory in the present context. It has been criticized by Berkeley, although it has found important restatements in contemporary philosophy.[19] Here it is sufficient to point out the role the causal theory of perception could play in the discussion about the possibility of experiences of God *and* draw attention to some weaknesses in the theory.

An inference involving an analysis of experience which comes close to the causal theory of perception can be formulated in the following way:

(1) "A experiences (has an experience of) x" implies that "x exercises a causal effect upon A."
(2) God is not a thing among other things and God cannot cause human beings to have experiences of God.
(3) It is not the case that A experiences (has an experience of) God.

The second premise (2) would deserve a more extensive discussion. In the present context it is sufficient to note the following: it is anthropomorphism to say that God is a cause without some kind of qualification of such a claim. Yet, it is possible to say that God is a cause in an analogical way, i.e. there is a certain resemblance between the way God is related to the world and the way—for example—a human being is related to the world. Human actions can serve as a starting-point for an understanding of divine actions. But it is far from clear how this analogy is to be developed. It is, therefore, not clear how the conception of God as a "cause" could be integrated in a logical inference.

But even if the status of premise (2) is unclear, it is easier to decide upon the truth of premise (1). It is easy to show that *many* (intentional) experiences stand in a causal relationship to that which is experienced. I have an experience of a tree outside my window, because there is a tree outside my window and it is somehow causally responsible for my experience of it. But it is quite another thing to claim *in general* that an experience of *x* cannot be an experience of *x* unless *x* is causing the experience of *x*. In other words: is it not possible that an experience which is an experience of *x* according to an internal description is also an experience of *x* according to an external description, *even if some other thing than x is causally responsible for the experience*? We shall return to this question in chapter 7, but let me already at this stage say that I am inclined to think that the answer to this question is: yes, it is possible. My experience of my wife having certain character traits is (says my psychoanalyst) caused by certain experiences of my mother in my childhood. It so happens that my wife has these qualities. But the presence of these qualities is not the cause of my experience of my wife having these qualities. Similarly, (certain) experiences of God may not only internally, but also externally, be experiences of God even if those experiences are caused by, say, psychological factors. In sum: the argument from the causal theory of perception fails because the causal theory of perception cannot be a correct analysis of *all* experiences (of God).

Is it possible to experience metaphysical entities?

Some philosophers have proposed that every view which distinguishes between different realities (absolute – relative, appearance – reality) or between different levels of reality should be called metaphysical.[20] According to this definition ontological dualism is a metaphysical view. Ontological dualism is an answer to the question what entities the world basically is made of. The answer is (roughly): matter and mind. A developed theory of ontological dualism is found in the thinking of Descartes. Some philosophers have argued that this form of ontological dualism is basic to the whole Jewish-Christian tradition. This means that one cannot be a Christian or a Jew and at the same time deny ontological dualism, i.e. the basic difference between God and the world. (In the present context I will disregard the fact that most Christian theologians would argue that God belongs to a third ontological category—or even a fourth if we think that ideas belong to a specific ontological category—

51

besides matter and mind. The following argument can be reconstructed in terms of such a more complicated ontology.)

T.S. Miles has argued against the claims (1) that ontological dualism is theoretically intelligible and (2) that the world-view of Christianity is necessarily dualistic.[21] In other words: Miles supports premise (1), but denies premise (2) in the following inference:

(1) "*A* experiences (has an experience of) *x*" implies that "*x* is not metaphysical entity (i.e. that the description of *x* presupposes ontological dualism)."
(2) God is a metaphysical entity.
(3) It is not the case that *A* experiences (has an experience of) God.

But why is it theoretically unintelligible to conceive of metaphysical entities and especially realities which are described in terms of material or spiritual? Miles claims that ontological dualism can be adequately understood as an answer to the following question: what basic entities do really exist in the universe? But the person who poses such a question is guilty of the *absolute existence-mistake*. Questions about "existence" are possible only in a particular context. A person might ask "what is for supper?" or "does there exist a prime number between 25 and 30?" But to ask "what kinds of entities really exist in the universe?" (as Descartes and many other philosophers have done) where no context at all has been or could be given is to mislead ourselves with words. Such questions are misleading because they presuppose that we can give an ontologically ultimate definition of the kinds of things which "really exist"—which we cannot. And the answers to such questions are also misleading (including the one given by Descartes): ". . . any answer. . . is inappropriate; it is equally incorrect to assert that only 'material' realities exist and to assert that 'non-material' or 'spiritual' realities exist in addition."[22]

Says Miles:

> If . . . it is a mistake to ask whether there exists a 'non-material' or 'spiritual' world in addition to 'the material world', then it is also a mistake to suppose that religious experience puts people in touch with such a world.[23]

(Miles also has another argument for the emptiness of all assertions concerning a 'non-material' Being. This seems to be an argument from some kind of empiricist criterion of meaningfulness, but we shall not assess this argument in the present context.[24])

Miles' argument merits closer inspection. We can begin by formulating the following three questions:

Question 1: does the Loch Ness monster really exist?

Question 2: do physical objects really exist?
Question 3: does anything besides physical objects really exist?

The first question is—according to Miles—quite in order. But the second and third questions are mistaken or misleading. To ask such questions is to make the absolute existence-mistake, i.e. presupposing the existence of an ontologically ultimate definition of "really exist". But no such definition is possible.

Miles' analysis is not entirely convincing. He analyses question 2 and question 3 in the same way, but he does not attend to the fact that while question 2 immediately strikes us as extremely odd and eccentric, this is not the case with question 3. There is, I think another analysis of these questions, which does justice to this difference between the two questions. This analysis makes use of an analysis of "existence" and "reality" emphasized by Konrad Marc-Wogau:

"Existierend" oder "wirklich" werden dem "Unwirklichen" als etwas "nur Vorstelltem", "Halluziniertem" oder "Imaginären" entgegengestellt. Z.B.: "Löwen existieren, Zentauren existieren dagegen nicht."[25]

This analysis can be applied in the present context in the following way. If "really exist" is contrasted to imagined, hallucinated or dreamt, then the oddity of the question "do physical objects really exist?" becomes clear. It is indeed eccentric to suggest that physical objects (nota bene: not a particular physical object as in question 1) are merely imagined, hallucinated or dreamt. But to ask the question whether anything besides physical objects "really exist", i.e. whether the experience of anything besides physical objects is mere imagination or hallucination, is certainly not odd in any comparable way.

If this is correct, then Miles' view of question 3 as being "misguided" or "misleading" becomes quite unjustified. To ask whether there exists anything besides physical objects—for example, minds, ideas or gods—is to express an uncertainty whether these things are merely imagined or not.

In sum: even if x is a metaphysical entity, it does not follow that it is impossible to experience x.

On the other hand, I think Miles is correct when he claims that Jewish-Christian tradition has not always described God as a metaphysical entity. There are examples of theologians who have tried to conceive as the starting point of theology an ontology other than ontological dualism. One such example is Paul Tillich. Tillich claims that God does not exist as a supernatural Being outside the empirical world. God exists in this world as "the Ground of Being".[26] The symbol of "depth" is more adequate when it comes to God than the symbol of "height". Many thinkers have argued that nothing is gained in this shift. Metaphysical thinking is still present in disguise. But these critics overlook the fact that another set of questions become relevant if we prefer the metaphor of depth to the metaphor of height.[27]

53

Conclusion

I have argued that even if there are arguments against the possibility of experiencing God, none of these arguments are free from weaknesses. Needless to say, there might be other arguments which are better, but I fail to see what these arguments could be.

My tentative conclusion is therefore, that experiences of God are possible. Such a conclusion is important to the rationality of theism. But there is another question closely related to the possibility of experiences of God and of equal importance in the theistic world-view, namely the question about the possibility of experiencing a revelation from God. What does it mean to say that God has revealed God's self? Is it possible to justify such a claim or do we simply have to accept it on authority? These questions will be discussed in the next chapter.

NOTES

[1] Unger 1984.
[2] Price 1964, pp. 22 f.
[3] Hepburn 1966, pp. 56 f.
[4] Hick 1973, p. 94.
[5] Ibid.
[6] Gilkey 1982, p. 78 has an interesting discussion about this problem in terms of God's "self-limitation".
[7] Stace 1969, pp. 47 and 48.
[8] Becker 1971, p. 67.
[9] Stace 1969, p. 48.
[10] Lyttkens 1979, p. 213. On the relation between parapsychological and religious experiences, see Forell 1968.
[11] Oakes 1981, p. 364.
[12] Oakes 1981, p. 363.
[13] At this point we are confronted with the whole problem of the relationship between God and time. On this see e.g. Pike 1970; Pike argues that it is impossible to conceive God being 'beyond time' (given a theistic concept of God).
[13a] Lyttkens 1979, p. 215.
[14] See Jeffner 1979, pp. 251 f.
[15] Ramsey 1957, p. 15.
[16] Lyttkens 1979, p. 213.
[17] Hudson 1979, p. 197.
[18] See further in chapter 1, pp. 20 f.
[19] See Grice 1968, pp. 85–112.
[20] See, for example Hamlyn 1984, chapter 1.
[21] Miles 1972, p. 31, pp. 40 ff. and pp. 49 ff. For another critique of Miles' argument, see Helm 1977.
[22] See Miles 1972, pp. 23–26.—The last quotation is taken from p. 26.
[23] Miles 1972, p. 27.
[24] See Miles 1972, pp. 30 f.—For a further critique see Helm 1977, p. 26.
[25] Marc-Wogau 1945, p. 70.—Marc-Wogau suggests that this is the interpretation of "exist" which is found in *Principia Mathematica*.
[26] Tillich 1964, pp. 5–11.
[27] See Sutherland 1984.

Chapter 4

Revelatory experiences

In his book *Religion and Rationality* Terence Penelhum asserts that there is one clear difference between the concept of revelation and the concept of religious experience. Revelation is a theological concept, but religious experience is a psychological concept. Penelhum means that the concept of revelation can only be applied by a person who believes that there is a God to reveal God's self. But the concept of religious experience can be applied by any person irrespective of his or her religious beliefs.

> Only a believer can hold that revelation occurs. Someone who does not believe there is a God to reveal Himself cannot believe this . . .
> To say that someone has had a religious experience of some kind is to say that he had a certain psychological episode occur in his life story. One can say this without having to accept either his, or anyone else's, interpretation of this episode. [1]

There are some points suggested by Penelhum's remarks which can be made more explicit. Firstly, I think it is fruitful to make a distinction between two types of religious experiences, i.e. revelatory religious experiences and non-revelatory religious experiences. This distinction is closely linked to Smart's distinction between numinous experiences and mystical experiences—with the qualification that the class of nonrevelatory religious experiences is clearly larger than the class of mystical experiences.

The main difference between revelatory religious experiences and non-revelatory religious experiences is that revelatory experiences occur in the context of a belief in a *personal* god. In revelatory experiences, the transcendent appears as a reality which stands in a relationship to the believer which resembles a relationship between two human beings.

But to have a revelatory experience, does not only mean to have a personal experience of the transcendent. To have a revelatory experience, implies having an experience of something "new". It is very difficult to make this implication precise. It is sufficient to note that the *newness* of a revelatory experience is not necessarily due to the fact that the experience makes us aware of something (not necessarily something about the transcendent *alone*) which we did not know. It could also be the case that we knew it—but did not want to "face it".

But, thirdly, revelatory experiences are distinguished by a further characteristic. To have a revelatory experience does not only mean that we have an experience of the transcendent as personal and of something which is in some sense of the word "new". It also means that it is the transcendent which *brings about* the revelatory experience. In chapter 7 we shall argue that a religious experience does not necessarily carry a conviction about the cause of the experience. But to have a revelatory religious experience means to have an experience which has been brought about by the transcendent. A revelatory experience is—in other words—understood as an act of God. And if it is not understood as an act of God, it is not a revelatory experience.

To sum up: a revelatory experience (1) occurs in the context of a belief in a personal god, (2) is an experience of something "new" and (3) has been brought about by the transcendent. George Mavrodes concurs with this analysis in the following remark:

> In general, then, a revelation is an experience that is brought about deliberately by its object and, at least in part, for the sake of the knowledge which the experiencing subject is to gain. It is not, therefore, hard to see why theistic religions, like Christianity and Islam, should find greater use for the revelation terminology.[2]

There is, however, still another distinction which has to be made in the present context. Not all revelatory experiences communicate truths which are taken to be essential for the salvation of humanity. Some revelatory experiences are not essential for the salvation of humanity—even if they are good for the individual and may serve to deepen the faith of a particular religious group. In the present context, we shall focus our attention upon the *essential* revelatory experiences claimed by Christians to be reflected in the books of the Bible.

In Christian theology, it is often affirmed that the books of the Bible must be seen as the outcome of a series of revelatory religious experiences. But the form of these revelatory experiences is a matter of theological disagreement. John Hick has proposed that a distinction can be made between those who affirm that the revelatory experiences behind the Bible are propositional and those who affirm that they are nonpropositional.[3] According to the propositional view the Bible contains fundamental propositions about God which have been communicated from God to the writers of the Bible in a supernatural way. On the nonpropositional view, the content of the revelatory experiences are not a set of propositions but rather God, who brings God's self within the range of human experience through certain historical events and, most centrally, those associated with the life and death of Jesus Christ. The books of the Bible reflect these events through the eyes of those who have experienced them, as mediating the reality of God. Let us first discuss some critical objections to the idea and veridicality of revelatory religious experiences (see I.). We shall then proceed to the question of propositional or nonpropositional revelation (II.). In a final section of this chapter (III.) we shall discuss the rationality of accepting religious claims made on the basis of revelatory religious experiences.

I. Objections to the idea of revelation

Basil Mitchell has discussed two forceful arguments against the whole idea of revelation. The first argument claims that the so-called *"scientific world-view"* is incompatible with the idea that God guides events or the minds of men. Mitchell's main objection to this argument is that "a clear distinction must be made between science and the scientific world-view". And he continues:

> The latter is not itself scientific but is a metaphysical position based on the extra-scientific principle that everything can be explained scientifically. Philosophers know this theory as determinism, and the whole issued is, and is likely to remain highly controversial.[4]

If the theologian decides in favour of determinism, then he or she ought to consider that the whole idea of God as a supreme creative will—ultimately derived from an analogy with partly free, partly creative human wills—becomes without an intelligible foundation.

Secondly, *Biblical criticism* works on the assumption that everything can be explained in natural terms. But there is a difference—according to Mitchell—to accept this assumption as a methodological principle, on the one hand, and erect it as a metaphysical dogma on the other.

Maurice Wiles has some comments to these points made by Mitchell. Firstly, he claims that the rejection of determinism and the affirmation of the possiblity of divine revelation is not enough. What is further required is positive evidence for affirming a divine agency in particular cases. And the evidence at hand is, unfortunately, too ambiguous. This is an objection which has considerable force. We shall return to this issue below.[5]

Secondly, Wiles argues that Mitchell does not attend to the fact that the successful use of methodological principles excluding a divine agency has made it unreasonable for the Biblical critic to affirm the idea of divine agency. It is an undeniable fact that Biblical criticism has had a "secularizing" effect upon scholars and students. This notwithstanding, it is nevertheless reasonable to ask if the methodological principles of Biblical criticism and their successful application *ought* to make us unreceptive to the idea of divine

57

agency in general. This is a very controversial question and Wiles has not said anything which has contributed to a decisive settling of the issue. I think that William Abraham in his recent book about *Divine Revelation and the Limits of Biblical Criticism* has shown that the sceptic is not *obviously* correct and that the argument from the success of Biblical criticism is rather weak.[6]

The diversity of revelation-claims

There is another general objection to the whole idea of a divine revelation reflected in the writings of the Bible. This objection proceeds from the observation that there exists an embarassing diversity of claims advocated by different groups and individuals to possess a revelation from God. Should not the diversity of these claims make us suspicious of the idea of a divine revelation as a whole? Is it not wise to least abstain from any judgements about who is right and who is wrong?[7]

This argument is not without force. But I do not think that the obvious fact from which it gains its force—the diversity of revelation-claims—is sufficient to dispose of the idea of a divine revelation altogether. The basic notion of conflicting revelation-claims needs some careful analysis in the first place. For example, William Christian has observed that because Christians and Jews mean different things by "the Messiah" they do not strictly contradict each other when the one claims that Jesus is the Messiah and the other denies it. On the other hand, Jews and Christians *do* disagree on the belief that "Jesus is the one whom God promised to send to redeem Israel."[8]

But even if a lot of clarification needs to be done, the basic fact about conflicting revelation-claims will, needless to say, remain. And the natural response to this fact is a heightened critical awareness when such claims are made. As Brian Hebblethwaite has underlined, revelation-claims are *not* totally beyond rational scrutiny (even if they have often been conjoined with a claim to be beyond reason). Says Hebblethwaite:

> The revelation-claims centred on prophets and holy books, and the doctrinal systems that have been built up on them, can also themselves be subjected to rational scrutiny for their success in making comprehensive sense, intellectually and religiously, of all the data that come to us through experience *and* history.[9]

To sum up, the existence of conflicting revelation-claims does not give us sufficient reason to reject them all. And neither is an attitude of agnosticism ultimately appropriate. Revelation-claims can be critically assessed and the fact that different revelation-claims conflict with each other, calls for such a critical analysis.

There is one other argument against the affirmation that God has revealed His nature and purposes through specific acts. This argument is already found in the writings of Celsus, but it has been revived in theological liberalism. The main thrust of the argument proceeds from the assumption that belief in a special revelation is inconsistent with the claim that ultimately significant religious truths are universally available to mankind.[10] But the affirmation of universally available religious truths is required by the idea of a just God. Hence, the idea of a special revelation contradicts the idea of a just God.

This argument presupposes that the occurrence of a revelatory event is wholly and solely dependant upon the activity of God. The human agent is, then, conceived as a passive receiver of a divine message. It is, further, not possible to make any distinction between situations which are appropriate for a divine revelation and situations which are not. But it is questionable whether any credible conception of divine revelation can be construed without reference to the contribution of the receiver and to the appropriateness of the wider situation. And the reason for this is that every relationship between God and man must take into account not only God's initiative but also human freedom.

To be sure, there has been influential theories of inspiration which have made God's initiative absolute and neglected human freedom. Billy Graham's words that the Bible is a book written by God through thirty secretaries can be taken as a good example of such a "theory". Mitchell argues that "the reasonable response to this is not to jettison the notion of inspiration altogether but to develop less crude and implausible versions of it." The analogy between God and the Biblical writers might *not* be the relationship between the manager and his secretary, but rather the relation between teacher and pupil, where the teacher communicates his message to his pupils in a way which relies upon their creative capacities.[11]

A conception of revelation which proceeds from these considerations need not come into conflict with the idea of a just God. The occurrence of a revelation is dependent upon a divine initiative, but also upon the willingness of human beings to participate. In other words: revelation is an event in which the openess of God towards humankind coincides with the openess of humankind towards God.

II. Can God speak?

There might still, however, be another weakness in Mitchell's position, which possibly could be a hidden source of embarrassment for Wiles. To be sure,

Mitchell (rightly in my mind) rejects all crude theories of divine inspiration in Christian tradition. Nevertheless, there seems to be a "survival" from these theories at the heart of Mitchell's thinking, namely the idea that God *speaks*. It is often argued that such an idea must be eliminated from any credible conception of revelation. Some of the arguments for such a claim are the following:

1. The idea of divine speaking—in the form of communicating supernatural knowledge—cannot be found in the Bible. Baillie cites such Biblical scholars as Kittel and Oepke to sustain this argument. They have argued that the Biblical conception of revelation is rather "God's offering of Himself in fellowship" (Kittel) of "the self-disclosure of God" (Oepke). But is this really true? Hubbeling cites a number of passages from the Old and the New Testament which clearly show that God does not only reveal Himself, but also propositions about Himself.[12]

2. It is sometimes suggested that the idea of divine speaking is associated with an anthropomorphic understanding of God. God is conceived as the heavenly superman, who reveals His nature and plans in a set of propositions to His creatures upon earth. And since God is conceived as having a body, there is no problem with the idea of God *speaking* to His creatures. But this picture is too crude to be taken serious by any reflective believer. And many of the Biblical writers clearly understand God as transcendent and incorporeal. This, however, creates difficulties for the idea of God speaking. If God is incorporeal, God cannot produce sounds by expelling air over vocal cords. But this does not necessarily imply that the whole idea of God speaking must be rejected. When the Biblical writers tell us that God has spoken (which—for example—the writer of the letter to the Hebrews does in the opening verses of his or her letter) then this must clearly be understood as an analogy. Some elements from our normal concept of speaking are preserved while other are discarded when we speak of God as a speaker. William Alston has suggested the elements that link divine speaking with human speaking:

> What is left is that God does something which results in the addressee having an experience of the sort he would have if some human being were speaking to him. The nature of the "something" is deliberately left vague. Since God is a pure spirit, it will presumably be some conscious mental act; perhaps an act of will to the effect that the addressee shall have the experience of being told such-and-such.[13]

3. Some people would, perhaps, argue, that the idea of God speaking rules out general historical criticism of the Bible. In fundamentalism it is clear that this is the case. God is taken to have spoken every word in the Bible. This has functioned as an effective barrier against the effort by historians to evaluate the credibility of the sources and discern the complex process through which

the Bible has emerged in the Judeo-Christian tradition. But even if the idea of God speaking has been misused in an irrational way by fundamentalists, it is nevertheless not necessary that the idea is incompatible with a positive evaluation of critical Biblical scholarship. God may have spoken through the prophets, even if there is every reason to believe that this divine message has been transformed through a complicated process of editing and interpreting the words of the prophet. Historical criticism could be seen as one important tool to get "behind" this process (even if it has been the faith of the Church that the Biblical writers have not distorted the actual words of—for example— Jesus Christ beyond recognition). In short: belief in the value of historical criticism does *not* contradict the idea that "somewhere behind the present traditions God really did communicate to particular people to disclose His will".[14]

The warrants for a propositional revelation

Certainly, there are limits to our understanding of divine speaking. This is not surprising. I would argue, however, that the idea of God speaking—in the form of communicating some cognitive content sufficient for discerning the acitivity of God in the world—is not so totally obscure, that the question of its warrants is totally beyond rational assessment. In the following I shall give two arguments in favour of a propositional revelation. But these arguments presuppose that the whole idea of rationally assessing revelation-claims makes sense. This broader and more general problem will be discussed after the following section.

A logical argument

Basil Mitchell has argued that a more traditional idea of revelation (which vaguely can be termed propositional) possesses greater theoretical coherence than other (nonpropositional) conceptions of revelation (for example, those proposed by Maurice Wiles and Gordon Kaufman). Mitchell illustrates his basic point with a revised version of Wisdom's parable of the invisible gardener. Wisdoms original parable introduced us to two men visiting a long deserted garden. The garden showed some signs of continued attendance, but there were also indications of the garden being completely abandoned. One of the men, however, remained convinced that there was a gardener at work—even if subsequent inquiries lead him to the conviction that the gardener in question must be invisible and intangible. His fellow-traveller rejects the idea of a gardener altogether. Mitchell revises this well-known parable in the following way:

61

Suppose we now introduce into the parable something to represent religious experience. One of the men, although he still does not see the gardener, has a very strong sense of the presence of someone whom he cannot identify with any individual known to him. This would to some extent support the hypothesis of the invisible gardener (though the other man might seek to dismiss it as a purely subjective phenomenon). But, if they found a message purporting to come from the invisible gardener, explaining what he was doing with the garden along lines that had not as yet occurred to them, this communication (assuming that it could not readily be explained away) would tip the balance decisively in favour of the man who had all along posited the existence of the invisible gardener.[15]

Mitchell suggests that the situation outlined in this revised version of Wisdom's parable is not altogether dissimilar from what might be the actual world in which we live. The Biblical writers looked upon themselves not as religious geniuses, but as instruments of the Holy Spirit and as receivers of a religious insight which was of timeless importance (even if we are their superiors in scientific knowledge).

Nevertheless, Christian theologians have felt reluctant to subscribe to the mediumship of the Biblical writers. The "scientific world-view", Biblical criticism and the crudity of traditional theories of verbal inspiration have contributed to this reluctance. It is, however, questionable whether it *ought* to have done so. And it *is* questionable—according to Mitchell—not only because the relevance of these objections can be discussed, but also because the contemporary alternatives to the traditional conception of revelation can be shown to have serious weaknesses of their own. To be more specific, Mitchell claims that the traditional view—needless to say, revised in certain ways—takes account of the conditions which must be satisfied if we are to ascribe an action to an agent. This is, however, not the case with the views presented by Wiles and Kaufman.

Mitchell claims that bodily movements are not necessary for the ascription of an action to an agent. So, God can be said to act even if God does not have a body. But there are some other conditions which have to be satisfied, more precisely the following three:

1. The unlikelihood of the event's occurrence apart from the intervention of some agent;
2. The event's contributing to some purpose;
3. The agreement of that purpose with the independently known character and purposes of the agent.[16]

In short, Mitchell claims that Wiles' and Kaufman's ideas of revelation are inconsistent, because they want to preserve the idea that the revelatory event is an act of God, but at the same to deny that the conditions for ascription of an action to an agent—in this case God—obtain. To be fair, it must be underlined that they make Mitchell's second condition central in their account of revelation. The revelatory events are those in which God's purpose and character are more perspicuously expressed than in other events. But their failure to take account of the first and third condition is—according to Mitchell—fatal: if the events claimed to be revelatory could be explained in purely natural terms (as Wiles and Kaufman claim they could), then talk of acts of God would seem rather superfluous. And if there exists no *independent* knowledge of God's character and purposes (communicated to the Biblical writer's), the Biblical writers would have no clues to interpret certain events as perspicuously expressive of God's character and purposes. [17]

If—on the other hand—certain events could not be completely explained in purely natural terms (such as the resurrection of Jesus?) *and* these events contributed to a certain purpose (such as the salvation of man?) *and* certain fundamental truths about God's character and purposes have been communicated from God to some of his creatures, then it would make sense to speak of a putative revelatory event as an act of God.

In a subsequent reply to Mitchell, Maurice Wiles argues that it is neither possible (because of lack of empirical evidence), nor necessary (to affirm a theistic faith of a distinctively Christian kind), to affirm a direct divine communication from God to man in the way supposed by Mitchell. [18] An apparent consequence of this would seem to be that the Biblical writers were in fact wrong about their relation to God and that theologians should give up their talk about revelation because it implies an idea of divine action, which has been emptied of intelligible content (Mitchell's criteria for identifying actions cannot be fulfiled). But Wiles argues that these consequences are only apparent. The Biblical writers were not *totally* wrong; they apprehended something true about God, namely God's creation, God's purposes and God's love. And their convictions were not simply a matter of effort and achivement; it was, rather, like poetic insight.

> And it is because I want to stress this element or receptivity in religious insight, receptivity of what is true about God and what God is up to in creation, that I might myself want to continue to use the word "revelation" in relation to my own position. [19]

A theological argument

There is a also another argument for the claim that God has not only revealed Himself through events, persons and things, but also through communicating certain truths to God's finite creatures. This argument is closely entwined with the foregoing, but it is clearly separable from it. It might be argued that the acts of God through events, persons and things are not discernable to an ordinarily equipped human being. What seems to be a miracle—such as Israel's rescue from the Egyptians through the Red sea—calls for extraordinary explanations. But from where did their monotheistic faith that the only God there is, saw their afflictions and took pity on them, come? "Why could not the Hebrews have come to believe in a god of the East wind, of a benevolent Fate, or any of the thousands of deities of unusual events that human religion has created?"[20] If God exists and has the character and purposes which Christian theism believes God has, then it is natural to expect that "as heavens are higher than the earth, so are my ways higher than your ways" (Isaiah 55:9). Given a theistic concept of God, it is natural to say that divine acts have to be revealed through divine speaking. This argument does not—as the foregoing—rely upon a particular analysis of the conditions which have to be fulfiled in order to make sense of the term "to act". It relies, rather, upon a particular concept of God.

Pace Isaiah, we may nevertheless ask if there are not certain divine acts, which—so to say—"bear their name on their sleeve" and, therefore, are discernible without an act of divine speaking. God acts in creating and sustaining empirical reality and this circumstance has appeared "natural" to many men and women through the ages without an act of divine speaking. I think that this is correct and so called "natural theology" bears witness to this fact. But this does not falsify the claim that there are *other* acts of God which are not so easy and perhaps impossible to identify without an act of divine revelation.

It is important in the present context, to pay attention to a simple distinction, which is not always attended to when it comes to the problem of revelation. It is one thing to say that an act of God cannot be identified unless God communicates certain truths to us, in the light of which the true nature of certain events emerges. It is quite another thing to claim that God's acts through certain events cannot be *justified* by other means than by reference to an authoritative divine message. It is one thing to discover the activity of God (in the work and person of Jesus Christ, for example); it is another thing to show that the discovery which is made can be justified by arguments.

Is it the case that the truths discovered by divine revelation can—subsequently—be justified by rational argument? Anselm of Canterbury assumed that *all* the truths revealed by Scripture and Tradition could subsequently be the object of proof through reason *remoto Christo* (disregarding Christ). Thomas Aquinas claimed that this is the case for only some of the revealed truths.[21] We shall not take any stand in this controversy. It is sufficient to notice that two of the most significant theologians during the middle ages affirmed that *rational assessment of revealed truths is possible* and that argument from authority and argument from revelation do not come to the same thing.

III. The rational assessment of revelation-claims

It is often argued that the whole idea of putting a revelation under rational scrutiny is preposterous. When God speaks, there is no place for rational considerations; the only adequate attitude is total submission under the divine will. Therefore, no one can stand in judgement on a claim that God has revealed God's self. William Abraham has clearly drawn attention to the weakness of such an argument (because an *argument* it certainly is):

> This move simply fails to recognize the actual object under scrutiny. What is under scrutiny is not divine revelation but a human agent's claim to possess revelation. To examine the latter critically is not to set oneself up as a judge of God.[22]

Another argument of the same species is the claim that rational assessment of claims to a divine revelation—and particularly the claim of the Christian church—are irrelevant, because the divine revelation guarantees its own truth. Karl Barth writes:

> If the fact that the Son of God became and is also the Son of Man may be known as such among all the other facts of world-occurrence, how else can it be but by His self-revelation? Which of all the forms of contemplation and thought that we know and use for the perception of other subjects can be of any avail in this connexion? What physics and metaphysics can even lead us to this subject, let alone enable us to know it—to know it, that is, in a way that permits us, as in theology, to see and handle it materially as a basis, and formally as an axion, of all subsequent reflection? What authority, even if it is that of an infallible Church or the apostles, can guarantee it if it does not guarantee itself in their witness? If it is in fact guaranteed, it is by itself, because and as it is revealed in the sense described. Otherwise it is not guaranteed. Otherwise we will be forced to admit that we have only hazarded a hypothesis—a bold and profound hypothesis perhaps, but only a hypothesis.[23]

In a forthcoming chapter we shall examine some elaborated versions of the idea of self-authenticating religious experience. We shall find several objections against this idea. Barth advocates the kindred idea of a self-authenticating divine revelation. I would argue that all the objections which can be made against the former idea can also be made against the latter. Barth would presumably claim that divine revelation is an objective event, while religious experiences are subjective phenomena. And even if it is impossible for subjective phenomena such as religious experiences to be self-authenticating, it is nevertheless possible for an objective event such as the divine revelation.

But the success of such a move is only apparent. Divine revelation might be an objective event, but unless there is some creatures to receive this revelation, the whole idea of revelation would become unintelligible. Says John Baillie:

> We must . . . say that the receiving is as necessary to a completed act of revelation as the giving. It is only so far as the action of God in history is understood as God means it to be understood that revelation has taken place at all.[24]

This means that it is not the question of divine revelation being self-authenticating or not; the question is whether the *experience* of a divine revelation is self-authenticating or not. And for an answer to *this* question the considerations made in chapter 8 are surely relevant. To be sure, this does *not* imply that a person cannot be psychologically certain that he or she has experienced a divine revelation. Most Christians are! But what is being rejected in chapter 8 is the idea that a person could be *rationally* certain that his or her experience is veridical on the *basis of that experience alone*. The experience being an experience of a divine revelation makes no difference to that argument.

The criteria of a genuine revelation

It has been argued that many accounts of revelation suffer from the weakness of concealing the wider context of beliefs and judgements, from which certain particular claims to a divine revelation draw their support.[25] If we presuppose that there are no epistemological arguments in general against the idea that a divine revelation has occurred (such as the arguments from the "scientific world-view" or from the nature of historiography), then the question emerges about the nature of this wider context of beliefs and if it is rational to affirm these beliefs.

Within this wider context, certain beliefs stand out as particularly significant. This set of basic beliefs—as we may call them—consists, most importantly, of the belief that God exists as a personal Being, that God has created the world and enlightened God's finite creatures with the capacity of thought and moral judgement, that God has revealed himself to the prophets as compassionate and loving, but also as righteous and holy, that God has intervened for the future good of Israel and that God will lead God's creatures to a fulfilment beyond history. These basic beliefs are—in their turn—drawing support from each other but also from other judgements. For example, the conviction that God exists as a personal Being supports the conviction that God has revealed himself to some of God's creatures. But the conviction that such a personal

Being exists, does in turn draw its plausibility from judgements acceptable to nearly all rational persons (if the claims of natural theology are to be accepted.[26])

It is also largely (but *not* wholly) from these beliefs that the criteria for evaluating revelation-claims have emerged. William Abraham has proposed that the evaluation of a revelation-claim would involve ascertaining the following:

> (1) the moral and spiritual character of the putative agent of God; (2) the effect for good that the experience of receiving revelation brings about, e.g. an increase in penitence, peace, humility, spiritual power, and authority; (3) the inner certainty and conviction disclosed by the prophet as to the origin of his message; (4) the inner consistency and overall coherence of the prophet's message; (5) the degree of continuity between what is agreed to be known already about God and the content of the prophet's message; (6) the capacity of the putative revelation to illuminate and deepen what is known of God from elsewhere; (7) the degree of harmony between the content of the message and the course of events that are its context.[27]

Abraham emphasizes that the use of these criteria is not equivalent to a fool-proof test for genuine revelation. But the existence of such criteria is, nevertheless, sufficient to refute the charge that the acceptance or rejection of a certain revelation-claim is beyond rational considerations altogether.

Experiencing a person as a revelation from God

Another question which cannot be bypassed in the present context concerns the Christian conviction that Jesus Christ as a person is a revelation from God. How is this claim to be understood, let alone justified?

First of all it is important to be on our guard against the endemic tendency in theology to circumscribe the limits of divine revelation. "To pick out any one act or activity as the essence of revelation is to miss the total picture, yet this is what has happened in the history of the doctrine of revelation."[28] A good example of such an unduly narrow conception of revelation is found in Joachim Jeremias' book *The Problem of the Historical Jesus.*[29] Jeremias claims that only Jesus' own words are the unique and sole medium of God's revelation. Such a narrow conception of revelation is implausible for many reasons. It arbitrarily excludes the early witnesses from the locus of revelation and conceals the insight of Baillie that "the receiving is as necessary to a completed act of revelation as the giving".[30] Further, it seems very difficult indeed to construct a simple criterion whereby the *ipsissima vox* of Jesus could be distinguished from the early response to Him.

There is, however, one particular reason for affirming the *weaker* claim that the person of Jesus Christ is the *central* locus of God's revelation. It is, namely, an essential part of traditional Christianity that Jesus Christ is God incarnate. (The intelligibility of this conviction rests—I would argue—upon a distinction between two concepts of revelation: the revelation of God as a *mere* message from God *and* the revelation of God as God's presence in a particular human being.) This is not the place to enter into a detailed analysis of this controversial doctrine. What is to be noted, however, is the relevance of this doctrine for the identification of the central locus of divine revelation. Because *if* Jesus Christ is God incarnate, then the self-sacrificial life and death of Jesus Christ provides us with a reason for believing that God is a God of love. Moreover, it may be argued that viewing the character and purposes of God in the light of the person of Jesus Christ[31] provides us with a new concept of the love of God. This contention of Anders Nygren's book continues to be valid even if his reconstruction of the Christian tradition as a continuing conflict between Eros and Agape remains unconvincing.[32]

It has been argued that this vision of God as Agape could find other means of expression, which are not dependent upon the doctrine of incarnation. Maurice Wiles has—for example—claimed that our apprehension of the self-identification of God with his suffering creatures is not qualitatively transformed by the doctrine of God's incarnation in Jesus Christ. The (putative) truth of the conviction that God has entered our conditions and our sufferings in a particular person at a particular time does not add anything to the more general belief that God has love and compassion for God's creatures in spite of their sins and sufferings.[33]

Wiles claims that there is no ground for claiming that the idea of divine love is qualitatively transformed by the idea of divine incarnation. I would, nevertheless, argue that there is such a ground. Consider the following rhetorical question by Nygren:

> For what else is the Christian doctrine of incarnation but an affirmation that God Himself has come to us here in this world of sin, and that His holiness has not prevented Him from entering into fellowship with sinners?[34]

Such an affirmation is regarded by many contemporary theologians as mythological. This is not a very helpful characterisation as recent discussions have shown. It may nevertheless contain a kernel of truth; but this truth is better expressed with the help of a concept invented by Anders Jeffner, namely the concept of indirect statements. Jeffner writes:

> A set of sentences located in a fictitious world can together have an important relation to the real world, even if no single statement is true when located in the real

world. The fictitious world created by different speech-acts may lead us to find something which is the case in the real world.[35]

Jeffner suggests that the narrative of Creation found in Genesis 1 might consist of indirect statements, which possibly could be translated into a direct statement about the real world: "Everything that exists in the empirical universe is created by God".[36] But there is also reason to assume that there are indirect statements in a religious language which cannot be translated into direct statements. These untranslatable indirect statements may nevertheless express something true about the real world, because it is possible that the objects of our experience can be structured in such a way which is impossible to communicate without the help of indirect statements.

It is not implausible to regard the affirmation that "God Himself has come to us here in this world of sin" as an untranslatable statement, which—indirectly—states something about the person of Jesus Christ which is impossible to communicate without the use of indirect statements. (The paradoxes haunting the doctrinal development in the early Christian tradition testify to this fact.) If this is so, then Wiles' claim that the doctrine of incarnation adds nothing to the general idea of divine love is seriously questioned.

This interpretation of the doctrine of incarnation takes account of the often noted obscurity of the doctrine. But does this obscurity amount to senselessness? Is the truth of the doctrine totally beyond reason? John Wisdom once gave some illuminating answers to these questions:

It has been said that once at least a higher gift than grace did flesh and blood refine, God's essence and his very self—in the body of Jesus. Whether this statement is true or false is not the point but whether it's so obscure as to be senseless. Obscure undoubtedly it is but senseless it is not, beyond the scope of reason it is not. For to say that in Nero God was incarnate is not to utter a senseless string of words nor merely to express a surprising sentiment; it is to make a statement which is absurd because it is against all reason ... The statement 'In Jesus God was incarnate' is logically parallel to 'In Nero God was incarnate'. The latter we noticed is not beyond the scope of reason. Therefore the statement 'In Jesus God was incarnate' is not beyond the scope of reason.
   And we may come at the same result more directly. Consider the words 'Was there someone, Jesus, in whom God was incarnate?' These words call first for investigation. Was there such a person as Jesus is alleged to have been? Was there someone born of a virgin? Was there someone who rose from the dead? Was there someone who said all or some or most of the things Jesus is alleged to have said? Did someone speak as this man is said to have spoken? These things settled we have only started. How far does the rest of experience show that what this man said was true? Did what Jesus said reveal what we hadn't known or what we had known but hadn't recognized?[37]

This is not the place to enter into a detailed discussion about the justification of the doctrine of incarnation. This would involve us in an extensive effort to answer questions of the type Wisdom has formulated. My digression into the meaning and justification of the doctrine of incarnation has, rather, served the aim of showing that it cannot be excluded that the doctrine of incarnation provides us with a *reason* for regarding the person of Jesus Christ as the focus of divine revelation. Needless to say, this has been the conviction of traditional theology. It has had far-reaching consequences for its development. First, it has had retroactive consequences upon the interpretation of previous revelations. The idea of a divine revelation through a divine incarnation, has "coloured" such central theological themes as creation, history and morality.[38] Secondly, "if God was incarnate in Jesus and if He is the same yesterday, today and forever, there is no possibility of God telling people to do things which are in sharp contrast to what He has revealed in Christ".[39] So even if the doctrine of incarnation is obscure, the consequences of accepting it are clear.

Let me just add one remark in connection with the quotation from Wisdom. Maurice Wiles has argued that the rationality of a theological interpretation of the person of Jesus Christ is dependent—among other things—upon the experiences evoked by his presence in the lives of Christian believers. The possibility of affirming the unique presence of God in the person of Jesus Christ has to do with the ability of this person to illuminate the lives of men and women in different historical and cultural situations, to enable them to discern hitherto unnoticed but important qualities of their reality and to integrate their experiences into a powerful and convincing *Gestalt*.[40]

In this chapter we have presupposed that religious experiences in some way might contribute to the justification of a belief in a revelation from God. But is this idea of taking religious experiences as some kind of evidence for religious beliefs really sensitive to the nature of these experiences? Are we not being misled by a false analogy from the relationship between ordinary beliefs and ordinary perceptions? This is a basic issue in the present context and we shall now proceed to a discussion about this important problem.

NOTES

[1] Penelhum 1971, p. 164.

[2] Mavrodes 1970, p. 53.

[3] The distinction between propositional and nonpropositional conceptions of revelation has been developed by Hick in Edwards' Encyclopedia of Philosophy s.v. "revelation" and in Hick 1973[2], chapter 4 and by Terence Penelhum in Penelhum 1971, chapter 14.

[4] Mitchell 1980, p. 105.

[5] See below page 62.

[6] See Abraham 1982, especially chapter 6.

[7] This objection is suggested by Anders Jeffner in his book *Vägar till teologi* (Ways to Theology). See Jeffner 1981, p. 66.
[8] See Christian 1964, pp. 15−16.—My exposition rests upon Hick's analysis in Hick 1973², pp. 119−123.
[9] Hebblethwaite 1980, pp. 87 f.
[10] See Origen 1965, pp. 391 f.
[11] Mitchell 1980, pp. 105 f.—But compare Kierkegaard (Bind 6) 1963, p. 19.
[12] Hubbeling 1981, p. 102.
[13] Alston 1967, pp. 169 f.
[14] Abraham 1982, p. 17.
[15] Mitchell 1980, p. 104.
[16] Mitchell 1980, p. 108.
[17] Ibid.
[18] Wiles 1980, pp. 112 ff.
[19] Wiles 1980, p. 114.
[20] Gilkey 1961, p. 202.
[21] See Hubbeling 1981, p. 18.
[22] Abraham 1982, p. 36.
[23] Barth 1961, p. 46.
[24] Baillie 1956, p. 64.
[25] Abraham 1982, p. 50.
[26] See further chapter 10.
[27] Abraham 1982, p. 38.
[28] Abraham 1982, p. 13.
[29] For an analysis of Jeremias' theology see Braaten 1966, pp. 74 ff.
[30] See note 27.
[31] St. John 14:9.
[32] Nygren 1966.
[33] Wiles 1974, p. 72. See also Abraham 1982, pp. 61 ff.
[34] Nygren 1960, p. 97.
[35] Jeffner 1972, p. 15.
[36] Jeffner 1972, pp. 40 f.
[37] Wisdom 1965, pp. 19 f.
[38] Abraham 1982, p. 56.
[39] Abraham 1982, p. 57.
[40] See Bråkenhielm 1975, pp. 176 ff.

Chapter 5

Religious belief and religious experience

The distinction between religious experience and religious belief has been central to theological reflection from the earliest times. It is suggested—for example—in the book of Job in the Old Testament:

> I had heard of thee by the hearing of the ear, but now my eye sees thee; therefore I despise myself and repent in dust and ashes. (Job 42:5−6)

The distinction between religious belief and religious experience is also suggested by the resurrected Christ in his well-known saying to Thomas: "Have you believed because you have seen me? Blessed are those who have not seen and yet believe." (John 20:29)

The contrast between religious experience and belief is vaguely suggested by St. Paul, when he distinguishes between the written code (which kills) and the Spirit (which gives life).[1] This distinction has a career through the whole history of theology.[2] The contrast between religious experience and belief is more clearly expressed by Meister Eckehart in the following quotation:

> Der Mensch soll sich nicht genügen lassen an einem gedachten Gott; denn wenn der Gedanke vergeht, so vergeht auch der Gott. Man soll vielmehr einen wesenhaften Gott haben, der weit erhaben ist über die Gedanken des Menschen und alle Kreatur. *Der* Gott vergeht nicht, der Mensch wende sich denn mit Willen (von ihm) ab.[3]

Rudolf Otto seems to presuppose something similar in the following lines from his well-known work *Das Heilige*:

> Es ist zweierlei, an ein Übersinnliches nur glauben oder es auch erleben, vom heiligen Ideen haben oder es als ein Wirkendes, Waltendes, wirkend in Erscheinung tretendes auch gewahr werden und vernehmen.[4]

Finally, we might add the following quotation from William James' book *The Varieties of Religious Experience*:

> We may now lay it down as certain that in the distinctively religious sphere of experience, many persons (how many we cannot tell) possess the objects of their

belief, not in the form of mere conceptions which their intellect accepts as true, but rather in the form of quasi-sensible realities directly apprehended.[5]

The distinction between religious experience and religious belief has often been associated with a certain view of their epistemological relationship. Religious experience and religious belief have been conceived in analogy to sense-experience and empirical propositions, i.e. religious experiences support religious beliefs in the same manner as sense-experiences support empirical propositions. The following quotation from a book by John Hick can be seen in this perspective:

> It [i.e. philosophy of religion] studies the concepts and propositions of theology and the reasonings of theologians as well as the prior phenomena of religious experience and the activities of worship upon which theology ultimately rests and out of which it has arisen.[6]

This quotation suggests that religious beliefs have their epistemological foundation in certain religious experiences. (It also seems to suggest that religious beliefs have their genetic source in certain religious experiences—but this claim is not going to be confounded with the epistemological claim). This claim about the epistemological primacy of religious experiences implies a hypothetical view of religious belief: religious beliefs are hypotheses which can be verified and falsified by religious experiences. This view has, however, been strongly criticized by many contemporary philosophers of religion. In a review of the last volume of Swinburne's trilogy (*Faith and Reason*, 1981.) W.D. Hudson explains the difference between a hypothetical and a regulative view of religious belief in the following way:

> I think it would be correct to say that the central issue in contemporary analytical philosophy of religion is the question whether religious beliefs—or certain fundamental ones as 'God exists' or 'God governs the world'—should be thought of as hypothetical or regulative in character. Swinburne takes the former view. The alternative view is that these basic religious propositions concerning God's existence and activity should be regarded as methodological rules rather than empirically testable hypotheses. In this respect they resemble such propositions as 'The physical world exists' or 'Nature is uniform'. These latter propositions are anchored (to use Wittgenstein's word) in all the questions and answers of common sense and scientific inquiry. They regulate what counts as an explanation or constitutes an experience. Basic religious propositions, on the regulative view of their nature, fulfil a similar logical role in religious discourse.[7]

With special reference to religious experience Hudson further says:

> The logical role of basic religious beliefs is not determined by whether or not everybody subscribes to them; nor yet again, by whether or not certain kinds of

argument appear to some people to prove, or disprove, them. It is determined by the answers to such questions as: Given the way we talk about God, is it more coherent to conceive of religious experience as giving religious belief its probability, or of religious belief as giving religious experience its character?[8]

Hudson has defended a version of the regulative view in an earlier book published 1974 under the title *A Philosophical Approach to Religion*. Some arguments in his next book—*Wittgenstein and Religious Belief* (publ. 1975)—shed some further light upon his position. We shall divide our analysis of these and other arguments in four parts: first we shall look upon his arguments against the hypothetical view of religious belief, secondly upon some arguments for the regulative view, thirdly, upon a particular argument in favour of the hypothetical view and, fourthly make an epistemological remark concerning the regulative view.

Hudson's arguments against the hypothetical view

a) *Saving hypotheses in religion do not admit empirical falsification*

Hudson argues that the hypothetical view of religious belief implies an important analogy between religious beliefs and scientific hypotheses. But—claims Hudson—such an analogy cannot be upheld. Nevertheless, such an understanding of religious belief (in analogy to a scientific hypotheses) is implicit in the cosmological argument, the argument from design, the argument from religious experience and the moral argument. We shall here limit ourselves to analysing Hudson's critique of the argument from religious experience.

Hudson emphasizes that there is a logical gap between (a) statements concerning sense experiences and (b) statements concerning physical objects as well as there is a logical gap between (a^1) statements concerning religious experiences and (b^1) statements concerning God.[9] In other words: it is impossible to reduce a statement about physical objects or God to statements about sense experiences or religious experiences. So far Hudson seems to accept a similarity between scientific hypotheses and religious beliefs. But there is an important difference between scientific hypotheses and religious beliefs: it is always logically possible to save a religious statement from conclusive falsification by introducing an *unfalsifiable* saving hypothesis. Needless to say scientific statements can always be saved by the introduction of saving hypotheses. But the only kind of saving hypotheses which are acceptable in science are those which admits empirical falsification. *In religion, however, saving hypotheses do not admit such empirical falsification.* Hudson gives us the following example. Consider the following verses from the book of Deuteronomy in the Old Testament:

74

If . . . thou shalt seek the Lord thy God, thou shalt find him, if thou seek him with all thy heart and with all thy soul. When thou art in tribulation, and all these things are come upon thee . . . if thou turn to the Lord thy God . . . he will not forsake thee. (Deut. 4:29-31)

Suppose that someone does seek God, and, yet, is forsaken by God. There is, says Hudson, in the text a saving hypothesis to cover this contingency: "if thou seek him with all thy heart and with all thy soul". But this saving hypothesis admits no empirical falsification. There is no empirical test by which the efforts of hearts and souls can be measured. Hence, there is a significant difference between scientific hypotheses and religious beliefs.[10]

I would argue, however, that the only thing which Hudson has shown is that there is a difference between a certain kind of religious beliefs and a certain kind of scientific hypotheses. To be sure, beliefs concerning an *unexceptionable* relationship between the fulfilment of certain conditions and certain religious experiences are often saved by the introduction of unfalsifiable saving hypotheses.[11] The character of such beliefs differs significantly from the character of hypotheses developed in natural science. Many philosophers of religion have, however, pointed out that certain basic religious beliefs—for example, the belief that God exists—in certain important respects resembles hypotheses developed in human sciences. Basil Mitchell argues that reasoning in critical exegesis of literary texts resembles theological arguments. We shall return to this argument below.

b) *Religious beliefs are not precise enough to be regarded as hypotheses*

Hudson claims that there is a further difference between scientific enquiry and religious belief: the predictions with which the scientist tests his theories are required to be sufficiently precise to be tested experimentally.[12]

> That is, the exact conditions under which the test needs to be made can be specified and exactly what will happen, if the theory is confirmed, can be forecast. In religion the demand for this kind of experimental precision seems frequently to be evaded. There is an attempt to have it both ways: to claim that one is arguing from experience like a scientist, but to be vague about precisely what experience one is arguing from.[13]

Hudson appears to be on firmer ground with this observation. Religious beliefs often involve large-scale assumptions about the character of the universe, e.g. that the empirical world is the creation of God. Such assumptions are simply considered "too large for science". I think that Hudson is correct when he says that religious belief is distorted to something other than itself, if it is assumed that "the experiences which test it can be specified precisely".[14] They cannot. But this does *not* imply that there are no rational arguments in religion. Arguments in religion might not meet the stringent standards for arguments in science—but from this one is not justified in concluding that religious enquiry is completely irrational or that religious experiences are without importance when religious beliefs are assessed. It is certainly true that religious believers often refuse to surrender their beliefs in the face of falsifying evidence. Hudson claims that "this makes religion very different from science".[15] But this is not evident. A scientist does not and ought not to view established knowledge within his own branch of science in merely a tentative and provisional fashion. He may and should regard particular hypotheses in such a way, but not (as Basil Mitchell has convincingly argued) the basic tenets of the theoretical system of concepts and claims which he or she inherits form the scientific community. Radical transformations do occur from time to time in particular sciences—and we should expect them to do so even in the future. But the ground for an alternative system is not laid by discarding the traditional one whenever it is strained by certain observations and experiences. It is laid when the intellectual resources of the traditional system are developed to the utmost—without providing an acceptable explanation to a number of particular phenomena. But these resources cannot be exploited if the basic tenets of "normal science" are discarded whenever there is evidence that threatens to falsify them.[16]

Hudson claims that "refusal to surrender belief, whatever the empirical evidence, has been taken by many to be a *sine qua non* in religion".[17] He evidently takes this as an expression of the irrelevance of religious experience for the justification of religious belief. But it might as well be taken as an expression of the wisdom of the believer in not abandoning large-scale beliefs about the character of the universe until there is obvious evidence that the explanatory resources of his or her beliefs are completely exhausted. Unfortunately, there does not seem to be any agreement about whether or not—for example—Christian belief has more to give than meets the eye of many secular men and women.

c) The hypothetical view presupposes that the question "does God really exist?" has a final answer—which it has not

Hudson suggests that it is not only the case that the hypothetical view presupposes significant analogies between scientific hypotheses and religious beliefs (which is wrong according to Hudson but not completely wrong according to me). It is also the case that the hypothetical view presupposes that the question "does God really exist?" has a definite answer. But—says Hudson—it is important to view this question with a considerable amount of suspicion. Hudson argues that even if this question is meaningful, it is not a question which has a final and absolute answer. And the reason for this, is *not* that it is a difficult question, nor is it because we have not tried hard enough to answer it. There is rather a logical limit to the finality of the answers to this question. Final answers can only be found to questions involving concepts which have a definite place within a certain universe of discourse. Questions such as "are there wolves?", "are there living creatures on Mars?", "was there a man named Moses?" etc. involve concepts which have their place within a certain universe of discourse. But questions such as "do physical objects really exist?" "does God really exist?" involve the innocent phrase "really exist". But where is the universe of discourse within which the concept of reality has a definite place? It would presumably be an ontological or metaphysical system constituted by certain irreducible concepts. These irreducible concepts would, then, determine the criteria of what is real in a final and absolute sense.

But—and this is the main point—the world does not inform us convincingly about which metaphysical system we should adopt. Hudson concludes:

> Reality, in a final or absolute sense, is not something which we can discover. In the final analysis what we take to be 'real' is a matter of choice. We have to make our own ultimate ontological decision; we have to make up our own minds what criteria we will use for the application of the word 'real'.[18]

Therefore, there is no final and absolute answer to the question "does God (or god) really exist?" This question is as elusive as the question "do physical objects really exist?" or the question "does moral obligation really exist?", because they all involve the concept of reality, which is irreducibly open to different ontological schemes (of which it is impossible to decide which is the ultimately true scheme).

This argument appears convincing—and if it is correct it is an important argument against the hypothetical view of religious belief. It is essential to the hypothetical view that the question "does God really exist?" is not only meaningful but also that it has a definite answer in the same way as the question "does the snow-man exist?" or the question "have Soviet submarines recently visited the Swedish archipelago?" have definite answers. It might be the case that it is difficult to find answers to these questions and that the question of the existence of God is the most difficult question of them all. But if there is no definite answer, then the whole endeavour of seeking evidence seems misguided from the start. But that there is evidence (however vague) for a certain class of religious beliefs and against another class is the essential contention of the hypothetical view.

There is, however, one particular weakness in Hudson's argument. Hudson does not observe that there is an important difference between the following two questions:

Question 1: does God really exist?
Question 2: when one talks about God, is one talking about anything which exists outside one's imagination?

When Hudson argues that religious questions as well as the question "do physical objects really exist?" are "systematically elusive to the kind of answer traditionally demanded"[19] he does not observe that there is an important difference between religious questions of type 1 and religious questions of type 2. It might be argued that *real* is an indefinable concept (or at least not an uncontroversially definable concept); but this does not imply that the concept of *not-merely-imagined* is an indefinable concept in a comparable sense. Take the following question: is talk about my dream last night, talk about anything which exists outside my imagination? There is, surely, a universe of discourse within which such a question could find an answer. Dreams are not about anything which exists outside my imagination. No doubt it is difficult to formulate the criteria which prompt us to such an answer. But the point in the present context is that our concept of reality *in the sense of not-merely-imagined* is not irreducibly open to different conceptual schemes like the concept of reality *in the sense of existence.*[20]

Let us now consider another type of argument against the hypothetical view of religious belief. This argument is not explicit in the reasoning of Hudson. But some of his claims come close to the following position:

d) *Hypotheses can be rationally settled by recourse to experience; religious beliefs cannot (logically) be settled rationally, because it is impossible to specify the rules for solving disagreements concerning religious beliefs*

This objection to the hypothetical view has been discussed extensively by Basil Mitchell in his book *The Justification of Religious belief* (esp. chapter 5). Mitchell admits that there is certainly a difference between the ways disagreements are solved in science and the way disagreements are solved in (and about) religion. Some would argue that it is a difference in kind and not in degree; disagreements in science can be solved through the application of certain specifiable rules of logical or probabilistic character. But this is not the way in which disagreements can be solved in and about religion. Mitchell's discussion concerning this basic view concerning the relationship between science and religion can be subdivided in three parts. Firstly, he points out that Thomas Kuhn has shown that there is a significant difference to be drawn between reasoning *on the basis of* paradigms and reasoning *concerning* para-digms. Reasoning on the basis of paradigms (i.e. high-level scientific theories such as the physics of Newton or Einstein's theory of relativity) are rule-governed in a sense which reasoning concerning paradigms are not. But, secondly, this does not imply that reasoning concerning paradigms is irration-al. The choice of one paradigm before another may not be entirely dependant upon logical and empirical considerations. But this does no imply that such reasoning is only of interest to the sociologists of science. Being rational is a rule-governed activity, but it is also a matter of trained judgement *without explicit rules*. Such judgement is required when it comes to a) specifying the rules and b) applying them to particular cases. Mitchell asks us to consider the problem whether all moral reasoning is basically utilitarian. A solution of this problem requires trained judgement without explicit rules. Is it the case that this moral theory does justice to particular cases of moral reasoning? Accord-ing to Mitchell:

> It is necessary to judge whether the doubtful cases are or are not cases of the type of reasoning in question. There are three possibilities: (*a*) the cases can be made to fit without distortion; (*b*) the cases are not genuine examples of reasoning; (*c*) the rules have not been correctly specified. To decide between these possibilities requires thought.[21]

Thirdly, Mitchell argues that a similar kind of trained judgement without explicit rules is required when it comes to the metaphysical claims inherent in religious beliefs (for example, theism): "It is necessary and possible to judge whether . . . they suppress or distort the facts or whether they respect them and render them more intelligible."[22] I think that Mitchell has been able to identity a requirement of rationality which many religious men and women would accept in their religious life. The challenge of the problem of evil is a clear indication of this.

To sum up: we have discussed four important arguments against the hypothetical view. Our discussion of these arguments have forced us to accept certain modifications of the hypothetical view. It is indeed a distortion of religious beliefs to view them as ordinary scientific hypotheses to be verified by religious experiences. *Firstly*, religious belief are more resistant to falsifica-tion, less precise and less amenable to scrutiny by specifiable rules than ordinary scientific hypotheses. This does not, however, imply that religious beliefs cannot be judged "whether . . . they suppress or distort the facts or whether they respect them and render them more intelligible." But, *secondly*, these "facts" are not only the facts of religious experience—a point which will be elaborated in chapter 9 of this study.

Arguments in support of the regulative view

I have suggested a modification of the hypothetical view. But such a modification becomes less credible if there are strong independant arguments for the opposite view that it is more coherent to conceive of "religious belief as giving religious experience its character". Let us consider some arguments in support of this.

a) *Religious experiences are conceptually loaded*

Donald Hudson emphazises the importance of this argument for the regulative view. His starting point is a general theory of perception. For example, he cites the following passage from Karl Popper's *The Logic of Scientific Discovery*:

> We do not stumble upon our experiences, nor do we let them flow over us like a stream. Rather, we have to be active; we have to 'make' our experiences.[23]

Hudson applies these general principles of perception to religious experiences. Religious experiences are always interpreted—and sometimes even "*made up*" by the beliefs of the believer, essentially the believer's belief in God. These ideas are clearly in line with Steven Katz' influential article on the nature of mystical experiences.[24] Katz claims that "the [mystical] experience itself as well as the form in which it is reported is shaped by concepts which the mystic brings to, and which shape his experience . . . the Hindu experience of Brahman and the Christian experience of God are not the same."[25] The patterns and symbols of "established religious communites" are at work "before, during and after the experience".[26] And he claims that authorities such as Zaehner, Stace and Smart have neglected this important relationship between the beliefs of religious traditions and the experiences of religious believers.

This is not the place to make an extensive analysis of the content and tenability of the thesis that religious experiences are determined by the beliefs of those who have them. It is sufficient in the present context to point out that this thesis can be interpreted in different ways and that the strongest interpretation of the thesis—that religious experiences are *only and wholly* determined by the preconceived beliefs of those who have them—meets with obvious difficulties. But even if the more extreme versions of the thesis that religious experiences are determined by religious beliefs are untenable, this does not imply that some weaker form of the thesis is incorrect. In this context it is also important to remind ourselves of the distinctions—made in chapter 1—between (a) propositional and nonpropositional and (b) interpretative and noninterpretative religious experiences.[27]

b) *Religious beliefs are formed by religious "pictures" which regulate the believer's life categorically*

This argument differs from the foregoing since it departs not from any kind of psychological theory about the relationship between beliefs and experiences but rather from a more general theory of how religious beliefs function in the life of the believer. Such a theory has been advanced by Ludwig Wittgenstein in his *Lectures on Religious Belief.*[28] Hudson is heavily influenced by this account of religious belief. I suspect that in the final analysis he would lay greater stress on Wittgenstein's analysis than on psychological or sociological theories about the relationship between beliefs and experiences. Consider again the way he formulates the central question of this chapter:

> *Given the way we talk about God,* is it more coherent to conceive or religious experience as giving religious belief its probability, or of religious belief as giving religious experience its character?[29]

Wittgenstein's account of religious belief could be said to lay claim to "the way we talk about God". As is well known Wittgenstein departs from the Christian belief that we live under God's judgement. The essence of Wittgenstein's analysis is that the difference between a person who has this belief and a person who has not is that they have "different pictures".[30] And to have or use a picture, in Wittgenstein's sense, is not primarily to believe in certain proposi- tions. It is rather to take a certain "stand" towards the things we know and experience. The "picture" determines our attitude to the things that happen to us and it determines the way we act in the world. Hudson writes:

> The proposition 'We live under divine judgement' 'regulates' the believer in the sense . . . that it *determines* what constitutes for him an *explanation* and what does not and it *makes* his distinctive *experiences qua* believer what they are. 'This is a punishment', says the believer; and that explains it and gives the experience its 'feel' for him *qua* believer as 'This is pneumonia' would not.[31]

Wittgenstein's description of religious beliefs in terms of "pictures" has not only the purpose of drawing our attention to their regulative function. Closely connected with this purpose is another purpose, namely that of directing our attention to the fact (if it is a fact) that religious beliefs regulate the believer's life *categorically* (and not hypothetically). This has been strongly emphazised by D.Z. Phillips. Phillips claims that religious pictures "have a life of their own, a possibility of sustaining those who adhere to them."[32] Religious pic- tures make use of the believer and judge the believer rather than the other way round.[33] And if a religious picture is discarded it is not as a result of being convinced that there are sufficient evidence against the picture. Such a change should rather be described in the following way according to Phillips:

> A religious picture loses its hold on a person's life because a rival picture wins his allegiance. This picture of the Last judgement may lose its hold on a person because he has been won over by a rival secular picture.[34]

Hence, it is not a question of reason for and against; it is a question of win or lose.

Kai Nielsen has made a forceful objection to this use of the term "picture". He claims that an intelligible use of this terms presupposes that we have some kind of independent access to that which is pictured: ". . . there must be some notion of representation in virtue of which there must be something which the picture is a picture of."[35]

Now, it could be argued that the use of religious "pictures" (such as the idea of divine judgement) may not presuppose that their pictured reality can be represented in the ordinary sense of the word (God is transcendent). Still it might be the case that religious "pictures" are indirectly "controlled" by their ability to "suppress or distort the facts" or "render them more intelligible".[36] In a similar way we may "test" an ordinary work of art. We are not primarily interested in the way a particular work of art has represented a particular situation. We are rather interested in the way a particular work of art may—or may not—illuminate the depths of human nature in general. Or in the terminology of John Hospers: we are not primarily interested in truth-*about* things; we are rather interested in truth-*to* life (in contrast propositional truth) in the following way:

> When we say that Thackeray's Becky Sharp is true-to life, or to a certain recurrent type of human nature which we find in experience, we do not mean that there is a perfect one-to-one correspondence between the character and some observable individual; nevertheless we do recognize that there *are* these recurring types and that they are probably more clearly set forth in works of literature . . . than they are ever exemplified in particular human beings. They are, so to speak, "more true than life itself", more revealing of human nature than any individual persons we have met.[37]

Consider a believer who believes that humankind is created in the image of God. Wittgenstein would, presumably, say that to have such a belief is to have a certain "picture" before one's mind. This picture regulates his/her life and action. This may strike us as a promising way of deepening our understanding of religious belief. Nielsen claims that this is an illusion: if religious beliefs are to be described as pictures, then there must be something which the picture is a picture of. But this is denied by those who have suggested this kind of analysis of religious belief: religious pictures regulate the lives of believers *categorically*—there is no question of the pictures representing something which, so to speak, could be compared with the pictures. But to use the concept of picture as an analytical tool without presupposing (on the contrary denying) the connotation of representation is like speaking of man as a wolf without implying anything about aggressive behaviour.

The only way out for the picture-theorists, is to display the way in which religious beliefs can be said to represent reality. It is at this point Hospers analysis becomes important. Religious beliefs—such as the belief that humankind is made in the image of God—do not give "verisimilitude", the ideal of pure realism. Religious beliefs might, however, be true-*to* life, i.e. "not to any particular human beings who have historically existed but to certain 'universals' or recurring characteristics and dominant tendencies in human nature."[38] Believing that humankind is made in the image of God suggest that *total* human depravation is impossible; there is always something of God in human persons. Is this true-to life? Does it repress or illuminate the facts of human life? This is an extremely difficult question; but it is not totally beyond reason. The use of the concept of picture to illuminate the character of religious belief forces us to recognize this element of rational judgement in religious life. Religious belief may seem unshakeble—but the reason for this might be (at least in a significant number of cases) that it appears to the believer that it "fits" and illuminates his life—not that it shapes and adjusts reality to his or her preconceived beliefs.

An argument in support of the hypothetical view

The arguments against the hypothetical view are—as we argued on pp. 74–79—not conclusive. Religious beliefs may be more resistant to falsification, less precise and less amenable to scrutiny by specifiable rules than ordinary scientific hypotheses. But this does not imply that religious experiences—nor other forms of human experience—are without importance in the assessment of religious beliefs. And, further, even if there is every reason to believe that religious experiences are formed by the underlying religious tradition, this does not imply that religious experiences are *only and wholly* formed by religious traditions. It is important to keep the socio-psychological perspective in the foreground in all religious studies. But this does not mean that this perspective should be absolutified.

On a general level, it seems reasonable to view religious experiences not only as phenomena dependent upon the underlying religious tradition, but also—at least sometimes—as a factor which can reshape the beliefs of individuals and groups. This has convincingly been argued by Ninian Smart:

> ... it would be indeed odd if metaphysics, considered as sets of propositions to be entertained and believed by people, should have the enormous effect of creating out of nothing the powerful religious experiences of both great teachers and ordinary folks. It is easier to explain a dualism between God and the soul by reference to the experience of prophets and worshippers than to explain the latter by reference to a current doctrine of dualism.[39]

In other words: many religious experiences are formed by the underlying religious tradition. But the religious tradition is not always the sole dominating factor. Some religious experiences have a more independent and autonomous character. This observation will be further developed in the next chapter.

The regulative view and the veridicality of religious experience

But let us—for the sake of the argument—assume that the regulative view is correct (which it might be in certain situations). Does this imply that religious experiences are not veridical? The polarization between the regulative and the hypothetical view might give us an impression of this. But this is wrong. Even if it would be the case that the regulative view is true—that religious experience are formed out of underlying religious beliefs—this does not imply that religious experiences are non-veridical. It is one thing to explain religious experiences in terms of, say, psychological or sociological factors. It is another thing to assess the epistemological significance of such experiences. And it might turn out that a certain type of religious experiences could be explained with reference to psychological or sociological factors—even if we should find it reasonable to say that these experiences are experiences of something real. Some thinkers would argue that the genetic and epistemological questions are entwined in a complex way. This issue will be further discussed in chapter 7. As an anticipation of the results of this analysis, I would say, however, that the regulative view is not incompatible with the claim that religious experiences are veridical.

Nevertheless, the sceptic might still have reasons to be unsatisfied. He or she might say that there are many other arguments against the veridicality of religious experiences. In the following chapter we shall discuss some of these arguments.

NOTES

[1] St. Paul's contrast can be seen against the background of Old testament texts about the new covenant not being written on external tablest of stone, but consisting of hearts created anew by the Spirit of God (Jer. 31:33, Ezek. 36:26).

[2] See Kasper 1980, pp. 174 f.

[3] Eckehart 1955, p. 60.

[4] Otto 1925, p. 163.

[5] James 1974, p. 78.

[6] Hick 1973[2], p. 2.

[7] Hudson 1983, p. 95.

[8] Hudson 1983, p. 96.

[9] Hudson 1974, p. 68.

[10] Hudson 1974, p. 71.

[11] We shall return to this problem in chapter 10.

[12] Hudson 1974, pp. 72 ff.

[13] Hudson 1974, p. 72.

[14] Ibid.

[15] Hudson 1974, p. 73.

[16] Mitchell 1981, chapter 7.

[17] Hudson 1974, p. 73.

[18] Hudson 1974, p. 104.

[19] Ibid.

[20] We have discussed this issue in connection with T.R. Miles' analysis of religious experiences of God in chapter 3, pp. 52 f.

[21] Mitchell 1981, p. 89.

[22] Mitchell 1981, p. 95.

[23] This quotation is taken from Hudson 1974, p. 17.

[24] Katz 1978.

[25] Katz 1978, p. 26.

[26] Katz 1978, p. 27.

[27] See chapter 1, pp. 18–21.

[28] Wittgenstein 1966.

[29] See note 7 above.

[30] Wittgenstein 1966, pp. 52–59. For a more extensive analysis of Wittgenstein's analysis of religious belief in *Lectures & Conversations* see Hudson 1975, chapter 5.

[31] Hudson 1974, pp. 20 f.

[32] Phillips 1970, p. 117.

[33] See Haikola 1977, p. 89.

[34] Phillips 1970 b, p. 74.

[35] Nielsen 1973, p. 36.

[36] Mitchell 1981, p. 95.

[37] Hospers 1946, p. 163.

[38] Hospers 1946, p. 166.

[39] Quoted by Mitchell from Ninian Smart's book *Doctrine and Argument in Indian Philosophy*, p. 144. See Mitchell 1981, p. 32.

Chapter 6

Can we trust religious experience?

As far as religious experiences involve an experience of a transcendent reality, they are regarded with suspicion and doubt by many men and women in contemporary society. But this suspicion and doubt may appear in different forms. One form of doubt is directed at the veracity of the men and women who testify to such religious experiences. It is sometimes argued that these testimonies are simply retrospective interpretations of an unclear and confused experience adjusted to suit a preconceived theological scheme. Such a view is advanced by Jonathan Edwards commenting conversion-narratives:

> Very often their experience at first appears like a confused chaos, but then those parts are selected which bear the nearest resemblance to such particular steps as are insisted on; and these are dwelt upon in their thoughts, and spoken of from time to time, till they grow more and more conspicuous in their view, and other parts which are neglected grow more and more obscure. Thus what they have experienced is insensibly strained, so as to bring it in an exact conformity to the scheme already established in their minds.[1]

It is clear that such a doubt about the veracity of religious men and women can be justified in certain cases. There are undoubtedly situations where one is justified in suspecting that a person did not have the experience claimed. There is a saying ascribed to Jesus in the New Testament that it is possible to judge the tree by its fruits. If a person reports strange meetings with God or Christ, but his or her way of life remains unchanged, then there is at least some justification for the question: is this person really truthful in his or her testimony?

But on the other hand it seems strange to entertain a more general doubt about the veracity of religious men and women. In many cases there are no special circumstances which could justify such a doubt.

Scepticism about the truthfulness of reports of religious experiences may have other sources. Is it correct to say that our memories must inevitably distort our original experiences?

Different studies on the retention of religious experiences give some evidence for the hypothesis that the correspondence between a retained experience and the original experience depends upon the presence or absence of a dissonance between the expected experience and the actual experience. If there is a dissonance between the expected experience and the actual experience, then our retention of the actual experience tends to conform with the expected experience.[2] But recognizing such sources of error in our retention of religious experiences is one thing; entertaining a general doubt about the veracity of religious persons is another. Assessing reports of religious experiences must rather be guided by a principle of benevolence. The point of departure must be that religious men and women are truthful in their testimonies of religious experiences (without forgetting the weakness of human memory in general)—if there are no special reasons for assuming the contrary.

But misgivings about religious experiences may also appear in another form than doubts concerning the truthfulness of religious persons. In fact, a person may be convinced that religious men and women are truthful in their testimonies to religious experiences and yet convinced that these experiences are of no value from an epistemological point of view.[3] That is: you may accept that a person has had an expericence with a certain content, even if you deny that this experience is an experience of something real, something existing independently of the experience and corresponding to it. Clear examples of such experiences are hallucinations and illusions. Religious persons claim that they have seen God, met the virgin Mary, heard Allah's call or been chosen by Jahve and in most cases we may trust that these persons have had an experience with the content they testify. It is not necessary to deny this. Many people may still claim that such experiences are mere fancy, with as little value from an epistemological point of view as hallucinations or imaginations.

Many religious men and women find these misgivings concerning the veridicality of their experiences very strange. An encounter with God is combined with a strong sense of certitude. God can be as real as the physical objects around us.

But even if this is true in many cases, it is nonetheless true that some religious men and women do have doubts concerning the veridicality of their religious experiences. Such doubts are, however, most frequent among men without such experiences, or without any intense or conspicuous religious experiences.

In this chapter we shall discuss some of the arguments in contemporary philosophy, which have been designed to support such doubts about the veridicality of religious experiences in general.

Religious experiences have no independent support

A fundamental argument against the veridicality of religious experiences starts from the observation that there exists no conclusive proof for the existence of spiritual reality, let alone God. Such a proof—it is argued—must be presented before the doubts concerning the veridicality of religious experience can be resolved. Religious experience cannot be considered to be of any epistemological value unless one has independently of these experiences proved that the putative object of these experiences really exists and that there is a correspondence between the content of these experiences and the qualities of the object. Such an argument has been advanced by Ronald Hepburn and Antony Flew.[4]

It is not clear what kind of "independent" proof would satisfy these critics. Flew and Hepburn are both very critical of the thesis that religious experiences are self-authenticating. This thesis will be discussed in chapter 8 of this study. Anticipating the result of the discussion in this chapter we have to admit that as far as their criticism is directed against this specific theory it seems hard to deny the cogency of their argument. There are always circumstances external to the experience, which are relevant for the assessment of the veridicality of these experiences themselves. If I see a tree, then my future experiences of the object which I now recognize as a tree as well as the experiences of others are, in principle, relevant for the veridicality of my original experience.

On the other hand, it does seem unreasonable to demand a proof of the existence of the tree (to continue the former example) which makes *no* reference—either directly or indirectly—to the experiences of myself and others. William Wainwright has pointed out that such an independent proof of the tree cannot be found. For example: my tree-experiences can be compared and checked with the tree-experiences of *others*. But it seems unreasonable to say that my tree-experiences cannot be veridical unless a proof *independent of the experiences of myself as well as others be given.* If such a proof is unreasonable for experiences of trees, it is also unreasonable for religious experiences.[5]

Nevertheless it does seem reasonable to demand some external support for the claim that (at least some) religious experiences are veridical—even if it is unreasonable to demand an external support which makes *no* reference to human experience in some form. We shall return to this problem in the chapter 9 of this study.

Non-religious descriptions of religious experiences

Another objection against the veridicality of religious experiences is based upon the possibility of redescribing our experiences. Looking at a dog in the distance I may decide that it is a golden retriever. Later, however, I might remember the experience and revise my opinion, when I discern some details of the former experience. I might remember that the shape of the tail and the coat of the dog was more like a labrador and decide that this is what I *really* saw.

In a similar way we might redescribe the religious experiences of ourselves and others. It has been claimed, that it is possible to redescribe all instances of religious experiences without the use of any religious concepts. This problem has been discussed above in connection with experiences of unity and numinosity.[6] For some people, it does appear possible to redescribe an experience which once appeared as religious in a non-religious way—without altering the experience beyond recognition. But from this observation of what is possible in particular cases, it does not follow that it is possible in *all* cases. For many people—if not most of them—the religious character of the experience cannot be eliminated without distorting the experience beyond all recognition.

The heteronomous character of religious experience

Another argument—also discussed in the foregoing chapter—has been formulated by Antony Flew. He claims that considerable doubt is cast upon religious experiences because of their heteronomous character. According to Flew:

> ... their character seems to depend on the interests, background, and expectations of those who have them rather than upon anything separate and autonomous. ... the expert natural historian of religious experience would be altogether astounded to hear of the vision of Bernadette Soubirois occuring not to a Roman Catholic at Lourdes but to a Hindu in Benares, or of Apollo manifest not in classical Delphi but in Kyoto under the Shoguns.[7]

Flew, certainly, has a point. Many religious experiences have a heteronomous character being dependent upon expectations acquired through a certain religious tradition. What has to be added is, however, that many ordinary experiences—judged to be veridical—have this heteronomous character. This concurs with the observation in the foregoing chapter that the regulative view (that religious beliefs determine the character of religious experiences) is not incompatible with the claim that religious experiences are veridical. This idea will be further elaborated in chapter 7.

Another defect in Flew's objection concerns his neglect of an important distinction introduced by C.D. Broad. (Broad was especially concerned about mystical experiences, but—I think—his observations can be generalized to a larger group of religious experiences.) Broad readily admitted that the interpretation of mystical experiences is to a large measure dependent upon the religious tradition in which the mystic is brought up. But such traditions can affect the mystic in two different ways. Broad explains this difference in the following way:

(i) The tradition no doubt affects the theoretical interpretation of experiences which would have taken place even if the mystic had been brought up in a different tradition. A feeling of unity with the rest of the universe will be interpreted very differently by a Christian who has been brought up to believe in a personal God and by a Hindu mystic who has been trained in a quite different metaphysical tradition. (ii) The traditional beliefs, on the other hand, probably determine many of the details of the experience itself. A Roman Catholic mystic may have visions of the Virgin and the saints, whilst a Protestant mystic pretty certainly will not.[8]

Broad's observation can be applied in the present context in the following way. Flew has, rightly, drawn our attention to the heteronomous dimension of religious experiences. But he has, wrongly, forgotten that there is an autonomous dimension to (many) religious experiences and that mystical experiences belong to this category. It is possible that many numinous experiences also have a heteronomous as well as an autonomous dimension.[9] These experiences are certainly dependent upon the tradition to which the experiencing subject belongs. But they also display qualities which are independent of the specific content of the underlying religious tradition.

The varieties of religious experience

Another argument, which is closely connected with the foregoing has to do with the varieties of religious experience. According to Flew:

> ... religious experiences are enormously varied, ostensibly authenticating innumerable beliefs many of which are in contradiction with one another or even themselves ... The varieties of religious experience include, not only those which their subjects are inclined to interpret as vision of the Blessed Virgin or senses of the guiding presence of Jesus Christ, but also others more outlandish presenting themselves as manifestations of Quetzalcoatl or Osiris, of Dionysus or Shiva.[10]

Richard Swinburne has discussed this argument in a chapter of his bok *The Existence of God* (published 1979). Swinburne makes some important points, which have to be acknowledged. Differences in religious vocabulary should not mislead us into assuming that we are dealing with different things. And even if this is the case—as it sometimes is—this must be understood as a challenge to a particular religious claim, not necessarily as a source of scepticism about all the claims of religious experience.[11]

One small point can be added. When comparing different (testimonies to) religious experiences and assessing the extent to which they differ, it is important to compare the same *type* of experiences. A rough distinction can be made between reflective and expressive religious experiences. Expressive religious experiences are immediate and spontaneous religious experience in which the subject is deeply emotionally involved. Reflective religious experience is a consciously assessed experience and cannot occur without a certain detachment of the subject. When assessing the extent to which different religious experiences differ from each other it may be important to keep this distinction in mind. There are considerable differences among the expressive religious experiences within and between different religious traditions. But it is not at all evident that the same overall picture emerges when the category of reflective religious experience is studied. (A similar difference can—naturally—be made between expressive and reflective experiences of nature. It is certainly easier to find agreement in the latter sphere than in the former.)

The unintelligibility of religious experiences

Flew, in the last quotation, hinted at another objection. He said that religious experiences are "in contradiction with one another or *even themselves...*" (my italics). The claim that religious experiences involve concepts and truth-claims which are not clearly intelligible or are even contradictory, can cast doubt on the veridicality of religious experiences. This objection is in a special way concerned with the concept of God.

The cogency of this objection depends upon our criteria of veridical experiences in general. If it is a (necessary) criterion of veridical experiences that their content can be presented by means of distinct and lucid concepts, then many—if not all—religious experiences are not veridical. But if we accept that there are veridical experiences which cannot be presented with the help of distinct and lucid concepts—which require the use of symbols and analogies—then it is still possible that these experiences are veridical. And an objection to a too rigorous criterion of veridical experiences is that it would mean that many experiences which we find veridical in everyday life would become non-veridical. It is not always easy to describe the traits of character of a certain person with distinct and clear concepts. A political event has a complexity which defies an exact description. But it would certainly be very odd to say that such experiences are—for this reason—non-veridical. Similarly, it would be odd to claim that religious experiences are without epistemological value because their content cannot be presented with the help of distinct and lucid concepts.

Religious experiences are not intersubjective

Another argument against the veridicality of religious experiences has to do with the difficulties in controlling and predicting religious experiences. Ordinary sense-experiences can be predicted rather well. They are accessible to all men with normal senses under certain describable conditions. Similar conditions for the occurrence of religious experiences are often suggested by religious authorities, e.g. prayer, sacrifice and good works. But there is no equally firm connection between the performance of such acts and the occurrence of religious experiences. (This was—incidently—the bitter discovery of Martin Luther, which led him to the doctrine of faith as God's grace *alone*.) There are, on the other hand, many examples of men and women, who have been "hit" by an experience of God without any efforts to fulfil any specific conditions.

This argument will be further discussed in the last chapter of this essay. At this point it is sufficient to point out two things: first, it is true that religious experiences in general are not intersubjectively verifiable in the same way as ordinary sense experiences. This does not, however, mean that all religious experiences display an equal lack of intersubjectivity. Secondly, it is clear, I think, that a criterion of intersubjectivity cannot be taken as a description of the necessary or sufficient conditions of veridicality. At the most it can be taken as a *characteristic* of veridical experiences to be intersubjectively verifiable. This caution in the formulation of the criterion is advisable and can be justified by the following example. It is a well-known fact that many people have an ability to see things not only in the character of other people but also in the character of the physical environment. They have a special ability of apperception, which in conjunction with an ability to express that which they have perceived, may make them great artists. Such people may notice something in the nature of another human being or in the shape of a landscape. These experiences are sometimes personal, but it would certainly be very strange to say that such experiences are—therefore—non-veridical. So the personal character of religious experiences can hardly be a sufficient reason for saying that they are non-veridical.

Two further arguments

There are, finally, two very strong arguments against the veridicality of religious experiences which must be discussed. These arguments will occupy the centre of the rest of this study. The first of these arguments bears some resemblance to the first point above. It is sometimes claimed that there are no clear criteria for distinguishing between veridical and non-veridical religious experiences. Therefore, there is a reason to doubt their epistemological significance on the whole.[12] In the case of ordinary sense experience there are clear criteria for distinguishing true experiences from illusory ones. In the religious case this is not so. In everyday life we are guided by the testimonies of other people, by our past acquaintances with things and people and by our established knowledge of nature.

I would argue that analogies to these criteria can be found in the religious field—even if the religious criteria are far from clear and not very easy to apply. We shall turn to this problem in the last three chapters of this study.

Secondly, there is the argument which proceeds from a naturalistic explanation of religious experiences. This argument may be introduced by reference to a passage from Walter Stace's book *Mysticism and Philosophy*. In a short section in this book Stace discusses the relationship between mystical experiences and scientific results.

Stace says that most mystical experiences are about such things which science does not deal with, i.e. the reality behind the appearances. But some mystics have claimed to have received scientific insights, i.e. new knowledge of truths within astronomy, biology, chemistry etc. Stace gives us some examples of such claims—and hastens to add that "we shall find every reason to regret that such claims have ever been put forward."[13] The main reason for this regret is that (many of?) the mystics who have claimed scientific revelation have been unable to give an intelligible account of their insights. Stace concludes:

> It seems probable that claims to mystical revelations of astronomical or other scientific truths of which the mystic can subsequently give no account are delusions which are in principle capable of psychological explanation.[14]

It is natural to side with this judgement and extend it to other—nonmystical—religious experiences implying new but ineffable knowledge about scientific facts. A similar judgement seems reasonable when the experiencing subject is capable of giving an account of his or her scientific revelation but it is clear that the alleged facts revealed, run counter to well-established scientific results.

Walter Stace speaks of mystical experiences revealing scientific but ineffable insights in terms of "delusions, which are in principle capable of phychological explanation". This phrase suggests that the defining characteristic of delusory religious experiences is that they are experiences "in principle capable of psychological explanation". Whether or not this really corresponds to the position of Stace is another matter. Still it raises an important problem about the relationship between science and religious experiences. Is it possible that science could provide us with such an explanation (be it biological, psychological and/or sociological) of religious experiences? Does it follow from this that they are illusions? In other words: is it the case that if a religious experience has a scientific explanation, then it has no evidential value whatsoever for the nature or existence of a transcendent reality? This problem will be taken up in the next chapter.

NOTES

[1] Quoted by James in James 1974, p. 204.

[2] See Pettersson 1975, pp. 81, 101–105 and 106–111.

[3] This claim must be qualified. Many religious sceptics can, of course, claim that religious experiences give us some kind of knowledge, albeit knowledge about the character of the empirical world. Religious experiences might increase our knowledge of human nature or even give us certain clues to the structure of physical reality. What is denied is, however, that religious experiences put us into contact with a divine reality beyond physical reality. In the rest of this chapter it is this lack of epistemological value, which is denoted by the expression "without epistemological value".

[4] Hepburn 1966, p. 37 and Flew 1966, pp. 138 f.

[5] Wainwright 1973, pp 276 ff. (Wainwright also discusses several other problems in connection with Flew's and Hepburn's arguments.)

[6] See above pp. 29–31.

[7] Flew 1966, pp. 126 f.

[8] Broad 1953, p. 193 f.

[9] See the quotation from Smart in Mitchell 1981, p. 32. See above p. 84.

[10] Flew 1966, pp. 126 f.

[11] Swinburne 1979, pp. 265 ff.

[12] A clear formulation of this argument is found in Jeffner 1972, pp. 108 f.

[13] Stace 1961, p. 278.

[14] Stace 1961, p. 280.

Chapter 7

Natural explanations of religious experiences

In his important essay "Arguments for the existence of God" (publ. in *Religion, Philosophy and Psychical Research*) C.D. Broad discusses the consequences of naturalistic explanations for the epistemological assessment of religious experiences. Suppose, says Broad, that it is correct that these experiences are connected with physical insufficiency and/or neurotic disturbances which are known in other contexts to give rise to delusions. Is it not reasonable to conclude that also these mystical experiences are delusions?

Broad is reluctant to accept this. And he gives the following reason for his reluctance: let us accept the basic premise that there are certain psychological and/or physiological disturbances which give rise to what we know are delusions. Let us further suppose that mystics and prophets really find themselves in these abnormal states. It does *not* follow—according to Broad—that their religious experiences have to be equated with delusions. Suppose that there exists a reality which exists "beyond" the normal everyday reality. Then it is not impossible that some kind of mental and/or physical deviation is required to release oneself from ordinary sense experience and come into contact with this hidden dimension of reality. Says Broad: "One might need to be slightly 'cracked' in order to have some peep-holes into the super-sensible world"[1]

Nevertheless, the following objection can be made. Let us accept the point that it is not logically excluded that what in certain circumstances gives rise to delusions in certain other circumstances gives rise to new and, perhaps, highly valuable insights. Given the existence of a supernatural reality, this is not impossible. But the sceptic might pose the following quite justified question: is not this supposition about the existence of a supernatural reality an *ad hoc* supposition? Is it not something we assume simply to defend the evidential value of certain religious experiences? (Needless to say, it is quite another question if mystics and prophets really display the "disturbances", which we know from other situations to give rise to delusions.)

Another attempt to connect the question about the scientific explanation of religious experiences with their evidential value has been made by William Alston in John Hick's anthology *Faith and the Philosophers* (publ. 1964). Alston's contribution to this anthology was an article with the title "Psychoanalytic theory and theistic belief". But—contrary to the title—Alston does not only discuss the relationship between psychological explanations of religious *beliefs* and the truth-value of such beliefs. He also discusses the relationship between psychological explanations of religious *experiences* and the evidential value of such experiences. His argument on the latter issue can be summarized in the following way: if there exists an adequate scientific explanation of religious experience, then God is not a cause of religious experience; and if God is not a cause of religious experience, then religious experience is not an experience of something real.

Alston's argument has been criticized by William Wainwright in *Ratio* (1973). In the following Wainwright's article will be used as a starting-point. But I shall reconstruct and criticize Alston's argument in a slightly different way from Wainwright.

Two interpretations of veridical experiences

In the article by William Alston, he says the following:

> ...it seems to me plausible to say, that the presence of x somewhere (not too far back) in the chain of causes giving rise to a certain experience is one necessary condition of that experience being involved in a perception of x.[2]

This is a central thesis in Alston's argument. Unfortunately, it suffers from an ambiguity. What kind of relationship can be found between—let us say—a tree and a perception of the tree, when it is a veridical perception of the tree? Is the tree a necessary condition for the perception? Or is it a sufficient condition? According to the first interpretation, the basic presupposition of Alston's argument can be formulated in the following way:

(I 1) if an experience of x is an experience of a real x, then x is a (causally) necessary condition for the experience of x.

But the basic principle in Alston's argument can also be interpreted in the following way:

(I 2) if an experience of x is an experience of a real x, then x is a (causally) sufficient condition for the experience of x.

Let us, first, take a closer look at (I 2).

Epistemological implications of a sufficient explanation

(I 2) does not look very promising as a point of departure for the sceptic. It is evident that "the real thing" *alone* cannot be a sufficient condition for the experience of "the real thing". The tree *alone* cannot be a sufficient condition for the experience of the tree. The air has to be clear, the eyes uninjured, the nerve fibres connected to the higher parts of the brain have to be in order etc. But it could be argued that "the real thing" must be *a part of* a sufficient condition for an experience of it. On the basis of this, the following critical argument can be constructed:

ARGUMENT A
(1) if an experience of x is a real experience of x, then x is a part of a sufficient condition for an experience of x.
(2) there is an adequate scientific explanation according to which the sufficient conditions for religious experiences are of a natural (biological, psychological, sociological) character.
(3) the existence of God is not a part of a sufficient condition for religious experiences (from 2).
(4) experiences of God are not real experiences of God (from (3) and (1); modus tollens).

This argument against the veridicality of religious experiences is not decisive. If we presuppose that religious experiences—or at least some religious experiences—are overdetermined, then (3) does not follow from (2). That an event or experience is overdetermined implies (a) that there are many different sets of sufficient conditions for a certain event or a certain experience, and (b) that different sets of sufficient conditions are operative at the same time. If I pass my neighbour's house and hear a shot and a scream and if my experience is not a delusion, then the experience has evidential value for the occurrence of a murder. This is still the case even if we presuppose that my experience of the shot and the scream was overdetermined by a shot and scream from a radio inside my neighbour's house, which—as it were—coincided with the shot and the scream from the real event. These conditions may—*mutatis mutandis*—also exist in the case of religious experiences. There might be a set of biological, psychological and sociological conditions, which provides us with an adequate and sufficient explanation of an experience of God. But these immanent factors might be present together with another set of sufficient conditions for the experience. The existence of God might at least be part of such a set of sufficient conditions. This might illuminate the following remark made by Hick on Freud's theory of religion:

> Perhaps the most interesting theological comment to be made upon Freud's theory is that in his work on the father-image he may have uncovered the mechanism by which God creates an idea of himself in the human mind... Clearly, to the mind which is not committed in advance to a naturalistic explanation there may be a religious as well as a naturalistic interpretation of the psychological facts.[3]

I think that this objection against ARGUMENT A is, in itself, correct. But the question is if the same considerations do not arise, which we earlier encountered in our discussion of Broad's argument. Surely, it might be the case that a religious experience of God might be sufficiently determined by a set of natural factors and still overdetermined by—among other things—the presence of God. If God exists, this is possible. But why presuppose the existence of God in the first place? Is'nt it the case that this presupposition has the character of an *ad hoc* presupposition? Is this supposition made for any reason other than to save the established hypothesis—that religious experiences have evidential value for the existence and nature of God? If not, the supposition that religious experiences of God also have a supernatural explanation as well as a natural one is—to say the least—a far-fetched and simply unnecessary supposition.

One further question might be raised: let us presuppose that God exists. What is the particular reason for assuming that religious experiences with a sufficient scientific explanation also are overdetermined by the existence of God? The *lack* of a sufficient scientific explanation would provide us with a reason for introducing the existence of God as an explanation. But what is the reason for introducing God if a sufficient scientific explanation is *present*? We shall return to this question in chapter 9.

Epistemological implications of a necessary explanation

But the evidential value of religious experiences can be criticized also on the basis of our second interpretation of Alston's principle (i.e. I 1)[4].

ARGUMENT B
(1) if an experience of x is an experience of a real x, then x is a (causally) necessary condition for the experience of x.
(2) if x is a necessary condition for the experience of x, then every set of sufficient conditions for an experience of x includes x.
(3) there is an adequate scientific explanation according to which the sufficient conditions for religious experiences are of a natural (biological, psychological, sociological) character.
(4) the existence of God is not a necessary condition for religious experiences (from (2) and (3), modus tollens).
(5) religious experiences are not real experiences of God (from (1) and (4), modus tollens).

Let us look at each premise in this argument in turn.

Premise (1)

What prevents a real experience of x from being determined by other factors than x? Suppose that my brain can be stimulated by a surgeon in Uppsala causing me to have an experience of the statue of Liberty in New York. This is an experience of something real caused by other things than the real thing itself. In analogy with this, it is possible to envisage that religious experiences of God are caused by wholly natural factors. But this does not imply that they are not experiences of something real.

It is, perhaps, possible to modify the first premise in such a way that the argument survives. It could be argued that an experience of the *presence* of the statue of Liberty must at least be determined by—among other things—the statue of Liberty itself. Similarly, an experience of the *presence* of God cannot be a real experience of the *presence* of God unless God himself is a necessary condition for the experience of God. Together with the premises (2), (3) and (4) (changed in accordance with the modified terminology in premise (1)) it would be possible to conclude (5') that religious experiences of the presence of God are not real experiences of the presence of God.

I remain unconvinced about the validity of the first premise of this modified argument, i.e. that an experience of the presence of x cannot be an experience of the real x unless the presence of x is a (causally) necessary condition for the experience of the presence of x. Let us assume that there is a thief in my house. Let us also assume that I experience that a thief is present in my house. But it is not the presence of the thief which causally determines my experience. I am agitated by an article about thieves in the newspaper which I am reading as the thief is stealing the jewels of my wife. But does this specific background to my experience make my experience an illusion? It is in fact an experience of something real! Similarly, a person may have veridical experiences of God even if God is not causally responsible for those experiences.

Premise (2)

Premise (2) is—as Wainwright pointed out—not valid. X can be a necessary condition for y even if every set of sufficient conditions for y does not include x. Wainwright makes this clear with an example: if I eat arsenic, it is (in a suitable does, of course) a sufficient condition for my death. But the eating of arsenic does not include the refusal to take an antidote. The refusal to take an antidote is, however, a necessary condition for dying from an intake of arsenic.[5]

Premise (3)

Let us, however, suppose that (2) is correct. If (2) is correct, then it must be the case that the conditions referred to in the scientific explanation of religious experiences, must include necessary conditions for such experiences. But then the following question arises: is it even in principle possible for a scientific explanation (about the genesis of religious experiences) to be acceptable if it claims to have determined that the necessary conditions for the occurrence of religious experiences are of a purely natural (i.e. biological, psychological and/or sociological) character? William Wainwright answers this question in the negative—and I do not hesitate to agree.[6] We can determine that x is not a necessary condition for y only by excluding x or varying the strenght of x, i.e. x is not a necessary condition for y, if y occurs irrespective of the exclusion or inclusion of x; neither is x a necessary condition for y, if the strength of y does not vary with the strength of x. This makes it easy to understand that it is impossible to show that the existence of God is not—or is—a necessary condition for a religious experience of God. We cannot exclude or include the existence of God, neither is it possible to vary the strength of God's presence. If we presuppose that there is no acceptable disproof of God's existence then it is not even in principle possible to accept a scientific theory which claims to have determined that the necessary conditions for a religious experience of God are of a purely natural character.

In short: a scientific theory that excludes God as a necessary condition for religious experiences is not acceptable on logical grounds.

Nevertheless, our persistent sceptic might return with his embarrassing question: why suppose the existence of God in the first place? Is there any other reason to suppose that God is in fact (and not only possibly) a necessary condition for experiences of God? Is not such a supposition an *ad hoc* supposition?

Conclusions

Once again it must be underlined that the discussion in this chapter has been of a hypothetical character. We have hypothetically assumed that religious experiences can be explained with reference to purely natural factors. Does it follow that those religious experiences are illusions? The answer to this question is no. Religious experiences can be veridical even if they have natural explanations, because (1) religious experiences of God can have a sufficient explanation in terms of natural causes and still be overdetermined by the presence of God, (2) an experience of God can be a veridical experience of God even if God is not a part of the necessary causal conditions of the experience (which are purely natural), and (3) it is not even in principle possible to accept a scientific theory which claims that God cannot be a necessary causal condition of the experience.

But these three reasons may not convince the sceptic. Such a person could argue that at least the first and third reason are based upon an *ad hoc* argument: God is brought in—gratuitously—as an (unverifiable) necessary or (overdeterminating) sufficient condition for certain experiences. God *might* be a cause of these experiences, but there is no need to consider this far-fetched possibility, because there is no reason to suppose that God *in fact* is a condition for these experiences of God.

But the believer is not without answers to this challenge. He or she could claim that they have reasons for supposing that God is a condition for their experiences of God. In other words: there are certain criteria which distinguish the set of *veridical* religious experiences.

But what kind of criteria would be possible in the first place? Before discussing this problem, we need to make a distinction between internal and external criteria for distinguishing between veridical and non-veridical religious experiences. Some thinkers would claim that veridical religious experiences display a specific quality, which is detectable only by those who have the experience. They say: religious experiences are self-authenticating. These thinkers suggest the existence of internal criteria for veridical religious experiences, whereas others would say that there are only external criteria, i.e. criteria which can be applied to religious experiences of others as well as those of oneself. In the next chapter we shall consider the idea of self-authenticating religious experiences. In chapter 9 and 10 we shall turn to the external criteria.

NOTES

[1] Broad 1953, p. 198.
[2] Alston 1964, p. 89.
[3] Hick 1973[2], p. 36.
[4] See above p. 96.
[5] See Wainwright 1973 b, pp. 99 f.
[6] See Wainwright 1973 b, pp. 100 f.

Chapter 8

The idea of self-authenticating religious experiences

It is often said that the insistence upon religious experience in theology is a sound reaction against a cold rationalism which aspires to deduce theological truth from the basic principles of nature or revelation. Such an opionion often arises from a vague desire for balance between experience and argument in theology. But many theologians have a deeper motive for emphasizing references to religious experiences. Such a motive is suggested by the following quotation from a book by John Baillie:

> It is not the result of an inference of any kind, whether explicit or implicit, whether labouriously excogitated or swiftly intuited, that the knowledge of God's reality comes to us. It comes rather through our direct, personal encounter with Him in the Person of Jesus Christ His Son our Lord.[1]

If knowledge of God's reality comes to us through an encounter with Jesus Christ, then, surely, such experiences must be of primary importance for the theologian. Nevertheless, he might argue that rational arguments are significant. It is, namely, one thing to consider the genesis of religious knowledge-claims; it is quite another thing to consider the justification of such knowledge-claims. And even if rational arguments are of marginal importance when it comes to the genesis of religious knowledge, they are of considerable importance when it comes to the justification of such knowledge. Logical inferences and rational arguments do indeed have a significant place in theology.

It is, however, possible to question this type of argument. It has often been maintained that when it comes to religious knowledge, the distinction between the genesis and justification of knowledge makes no sense. The personal encounter between God and man/woman which gives rise to knowledge of God's reality, is also the ground of our religious knowledge. The futility of religious doctrines and arguments is basically not an idiosyncracy of anti-intellectual religious believers, because "the unimpeachable foundation for theistic belief is to be found in 'self-authenticating' experience of God."[2] It is the purpose of this chapter to analyse some attempts to defend the logical possibility of self-authenticating experiences of God. These attempts have been made by an American philosopher of religion, professor Robert Oakes.

In three different articles during the seventies he wrestles with this problem. First of all, two more general points must be made.

Veridical and self-authenticating religious experiences

In order to be clear about the concept of self-authenticating religious experience it is necessary to distinguish it from the idea of a veridical religious experience. To be sure, it is one thing to argue that there are religious experiences which are veridical, i.e. experiences of something real which exists independently of the mind of the experiencing subject. It is quite another thing to argue that there are religious experiences, which taken by themselves are a sufficient guarantee for their own veridicality. In other words: it is quite possible to argue—as I myself would feel inclined to do—that there are veridical religious experiences, but at the same time deny that the veridicality of all or some of these experiences is displayed by considerations which pertain to these experiences alone. It is possible that the veridicality of veridical religious experiences can be justified by their specific relationship to other experiences (coherence etc.).

There is also another point which must be underlined. It is one thing to claim that there are some veridical religious experiences, which—because of *practical obstacles*—cannot be corroborated by other considerations than those which concern the experience itself. It is quite another thing to claim that such other considerations are *in principle* irrelevant, because the experiencing subject could never (in principle) have any justification for questioning the veridicality of his or her religious experience. George Mavrodes has argued that practical difficulties in corroborating an experience is not confined to the religious field. He gives the following example:

> I claim . . . to see a timber wolf in Rocky Mountain National Park. My friend hurries to the same spot but sees no wolf. What significance has this failure? Notice that . . . the wolf has some initiative in this affair. If the wolf does not want to be seen, then perhaps my friend will see him only if he is more clever than the wolf. Can I show him the wolf? If I cannot persuade him to be quiet, to tread lightly, and to sit patiently, then perhaps I cannot show my friend the wolf. This failure does not show that my claim should be construed as a "low claim", or that I did not really see the wolf. The world contains many things and not all of them are as inert as a piece of paper. To demand that the corroboration of every experience should be equally as easy as substantiating the existence of the paper is simply to exhibit a foolish disregard for the relevant facts.[3]

Similarly, corroborating certain religious experiences might be beset with practical difficulties. The conditions for religious experiences to occur might be hard to fulfil and if Christian faith is correct about God, then men cannot dispose of God as they dispose of material objects: God will be experienced only when God choses to reveal Himself.

So there are clearly difficulties when it comes to the verification of religious experiences. This fact can, however, be acknowledged *without* subscribing to the claim that it is *in principle* impossible to corroborate certain religious experiences, because the experiencing subject could never (in principle) have any justification for questioning the veridicality of the experience. The claim that corroboration of religious experiences is not very frequent in religion, gives the idea of self-authenticating religious experience a certain support which is—at best—ambiguous. *If* it is the case that such corroborations are rare, this might as well be taken to testify to the practical difficulties of corroborating religious experiences.

Let us now turn to Oakes' argument. It should not be forgotten that he is mainly concerned with the concept of self-authenticating religious experience—and not so much with the actual existence of such experiences.

Oakes' first theory

Oakes' article in *The Thomist* (1972) is largely concerned with some common arguments against the idea of self-authenticating (or self-validating as is Oakes' term in this context) religious experiences. Firstly, he refutes the objection of Ferré that impressive encounters with other persons, let alone the person of God, often turn out to be illusory. Oakes argues that if an encounter-experience is illusory, then it cannot be counted as an experience belonging to the scope of the concept of self-authenticating religious experience in the first place. Secondly, he argues that the idea of self-authentication can withstand the charge that only propositions and not experiences are subject to verification: experiences involve interpretative judgements or propositional attitudes which can indeed be subject to verification or falsification. And, thirdly, there is the argument that reference to self-authenticating religious experiences is just an irrational move of some believers to protect themselves against falsifying evidence. This objection is relevant only if the idea of self-authentication is impossible. But if the idea is logically possible, it is also possible that there are such experiences. And if this in turn is the case, then it is not *obviously* true that references to such experiences is just an irrational move of the believer. This piece of argument does in fact bring us back to the starting-point: can there really be a kind of religious experience, which taken by itself, is sufficient to guarantee its own veridicality?

There is, of course, one particular condition which has to be fulfiled if this question is to be answered positively: there cannot be any self-authenticating experiences of God unless it is the case that God exists. If it is true that God does not exist, then the concept of self-authenticating experiences of God cannot (logically) be applied, because the experiences belonging to the scope of the concept are ascribed the property of veridicality. This obvious fact is clearly noted by Oakes. But he makes a rather surprising move in connection with this observation. He affirms that metaphysical questions concerning the reality of God, have to be decided prior to epistemological questions if there is to be any proof of God's existence, because there cannot be any kind of proof of God's existence if God does not exist: "the epistemological question of the possibility of theological proof is seen to be logically posterior to the metaphysical question of God's existence".[4] Oakes' postulate that metaphysical questions about what there is, are prior to epistemological questions concerning *how* we come to know what there is, enables him to reach the conclusion that the possibility of self-authenticating religious experiences is a *contextual* question, i.e. a question which has to be answered within the context of God's existence. If and only if the answer to the logically prior metaphysical question is Yes, can the idea of self-authenticating religious experiences be logically and factually possible. According to Oakes:

> ...if theism be correct, then there is a transcendent God who, by virtue of the infinite power and authority indigenous to his nature, could see to it... that an experience of (or encounter with) him would be sufficient to guarantee its own veridicality.[5]

Within the context of theistic belief, self-authenticating experiences of God are logically and factually possible. Whether there really are such experiences, is another question.

I would argue that there are two mistakes involved in this defence of self-authentication. First, Oakes' postulate about the priority of metaphysical question to epistemological ones, is far from obvious. The Dutch philosopher H.G. Hubbeling has commented upon this in the following way:

> Man kann natürlich philosophische Erörterungen sehr gut mit metaphysichen Fragen beginnen. Aber dass bedeutet nicht, dass diese Fragen zuerst gelöst sein müssen, bevor andere Fragen gestellt werden können. Wie wir gesehen haben, liegen ja alle philosophischen Fragen gleichsam auf einem Kreis.[6]

In other words: metaphysical questions concerning the existence of what there is are in one way prior to epistemological questions. But in epistemology we are not only concerned with the question of *how* we know what we already have assumed to be the case metaphysically. We are also concerned with the question of whether we know that certain metaphysical assumptions are true or not. The conclusion of such a reflection might be that certain metaphysical assumption are true while other are false. But then, there is a clear sense in which epistemological issues are logically prior to metaphysical issues.

If Oakes' postulate is false, then the case for the logical and factual possibility of self-authenticating religious experiences remains open. But even if his postulate was justified (and the metaphysical question of the existence of God answered positively), his conclusion that such experiences would be logically and factually possible would not follow. If we assume that God can do anything which does not come under a self-contradictory description, then it must be shown—which Oakes has not shown—that self-authenticating religious experiences do not come under such a self-contradictory description. We shall, on the contrary find reason to claim, that bringing about self-authenticating religious experience does not belong to the things God possibly could do, because the whole idea of self-authentication is incoherent. Let us first, however, look more closely at a definition of self-authenticating experiences, which Oakes presented in an article from 1976. The definition is as follows:

> ... we can now *define* 'self-authenticating' religious experience as veridical experience of God which is sufficient to quarantee that the person having that veridical experience could never (in principle) have any justification for questioning its veridicality. Hence, since it is a *logically necessary* condition for self-authentication that the experience in question be veridical, it is simply irrelevant to suggest that any putative experience of God *might* be delusive. If it *is* delusive, then there is nothing which counts as a *candidate* for self-authentication.[7]

The two last sentences of this quotation are directed against the earlier mentioned objection of Ferré and others, that the idea of self-authentication is impossible, because it is always conceivable that someone's putative experience of God is illusory rather than veridical. I would regard this as an argument against the claim that the concept of self-authentication has application in the real world—and not as an argument against the coherence of the concept itself. Let us leave this point aside and take a closer look at Oakes' defence of the claim that self-authenticating religious experiences is a logically possibly state of affairs.

Firstly, Oakes clearly acknowledges that such experiences would indeed be a logically impossible state of affairs, if the existence of God were to be a logically impossible state of affairs. And even if this might be the case, it is far from obvious that it is.

Secondly, a critic of the idea of self-authentication might argue that it is *always* logically possible for the proposition "I have had a veridical experience of God" to be false. Hence, it could never be the case that someone could be rationally certain that his or her experience was veridical, let alone rationally certain on the basis of that experience alone. This objection falters upon the fact that rational certainty need not amount to logical necessity: "... the suggestion that religious experience can be self-authenticating in no ways entails that it can ever be a *necessary* truth that any person N has had a veridical experience of God".[8]

Oakes concludes that there are no good arguments against the logical possiblity of self-authenticating religious experiences. This does not, however, justify the claim that there are in fact self-authenticating religious experiences. Nevertheless, Oakes is convinced that there are and that it is incumbent upon others to prove him wrong.

Yandell's critique

This challenge was accepted in an article by K. Yandell 1977. Yandell argues that there is a set of considerations which suggest that the concept of self-authenticating is incoherent. Yandell claims that Oakes' definition of self-authenticating religious experience presupposes a triadic *evidential* relation between a person, an experience and a proposition.[9] To be more specific, Yandell claims that Oakes has the following definition in mind:

Experience E of a person S is self-authenticating with respect to proposition P = given that S had E, it is logically impossible that S ever justifiably doubt that P is true.[10]

If this is the definition Oakes *really* intends, then it is natural to ask if there is *any* kind of experience (let alone experiences of God) the having of which, makes it impossible to justifiably doubt *any* kind of propositions (let alone propositions about God). And the argument of Yandell is, roughly, aimed at the conclusion that this *might* be the case with such propositions as "I am in pain now" because they concern only the current content of one's own immediate awareness. Such propositions have marginal ramifications, i.e. given that I know them to be true, there is little—if anything—I can rightly claim to know about the world outside the content of my own mind. In other words: the self-authenticating character of—for example—experiences of my own pain at a particular moment is bought at the price of extreme exclusion of any kind of other knowledge-claims about "the outside world". Yandell concludes:

Roughly, the less ramifications a claim has ..., the more plausible a candidate for being at least momentarily self-authenticated a claim is.[11]

Clearly, ordinary claims of our everyday life cannot be confirmed by self-authenticating experiences.

... if I claim *I have a pen in my hand at t* to be true, it cannot be that the conditions for its truth are all "present to me" a *t*. For pens and hands are physical (and hence enduring) objects—if not substances, then continuants. They have dispositional as well as episodic properties, and non-ephemeral biographies. So *other* experiences are relevant to this modest claim, and confirmation of the claim is inherently open ended.[12]

So sense-experiences are clearly not self-authenticating. Yandell goes on to argue that in the case of religious experiences, claims to self-authentication are "at their lowest level of plausibility" because of their extraordinary wide-ranging ramifications. He says:

... for claims of a scope wide enough, and ramifications rich enough, to be religiously basic, further application of these beliefs... is likely to be always possible, now and later. So further checking will be possible. Why it should not also be appropriate is opaque... Concerning *God exists,* John Wisdom once remarked "to this question every incident in the history of the world is relevant—whether it is the fall of a sparrow or the coming of a harvest, the passing of an empire or the fading of a smile."[13]

The essential point of this argument is that it is logically impossible to claim that certain particular experiences (their veridicality notwithstanding) could be sufficient evidence for beliefs with such wideranging ramifications as *God exists*. We may grant that claims to self-authentication would gain some plausiblity when it comes to propositions with minimal ramifications. But then again, the proposition *God exists* could not possibly be considered for such a claim. It is exactly that proposition which is implied by the descriptions of the encounter-experiences which Oakes claims to be self-authenticating.

Oakes' later theory about necessarily veridical experiences

In another article from 1979 Oakes makes a third effort to convince us about the possibility of self-authenticating religious experiences. This time he approaches the problem from a new angle. He argues from an essentialist position and subscribes to the doctrine that particulars have some (but not all) of their properties essentially (necessarily) rather than accidentally (contingently). "Hence, given any particular that you please, some of its properties (e.g., being self-identical) are such that just the *existence* of that particular is logically sufficient for its having them".[14] This leads Oakes to the idea of experiences having the property of *being necessarily veridical*. He argues that it is not inconceivable that there are such experiences. There are, undoubtedly, propositions with the property of *being necessarily true*. Hence, it is reasonable to assume that there are experiences which have analogous properties.[15]

Let us presuppose that Oakes' case is satisfactory so far and bypass the possible weaknesses in his argument from analogy. Let us, further, assume that the idea of experiences having the property of being necessarily veridical is logically possible and, moreover, that there exist experiences with such a property. *The next step* in Oakes' argument is then to establish that self-authenticating experiences can be analysed as experiences being necessarily veridical. If this is not established, nothing is gained by the introduction of the essentialist terminology in the present context. To this end, Oakes suggests a new definition of the concept of self-authenticating experience:

> An experience (*E*) had by some person (*N*) is self-authenticating (guarantees its veridicality to *N*) iff (a) *E* is veridical and (b) *N*'s *belief* that *E* is veridical is logically sufficient for *N*'s *knowing* (in the very strongest sense, i.e., *being certain*) that *E* is veridical; another way of putting (b), of course, is that it would be logically impossible for *N* both to believe that *E* is veridical and not be certain that it is. [16]

Presupposing this definition, Oakes claims that a self-authenticating experience can indeed be analyzed as a necessarily veridical experience. Nothing could possibly be required to certify the veridicality of an experience— assumed to be self-authenticating—other than its being an experience with the property of being necessarily veridical.

> Hence, for any veridical experience to which veridicality was essential, I conclude that it would be inconceivable for any person who had such an experience to believe (truly, of course) that it was veridical and not know (i.e. be certain) that it was. If this is correct, then "*E* is an experience to which veridicality is essential" entails "*E* is an experience that is self-authenticating". Since it is clear, however, that the former proposition is entailed by the latter, the propositions in question are logically equivalent. [17]

The third and last step in this argument to undermine the resistance to the idea of self-authenticating religious experiences, is to strengthen the credibility of the idea that such experiences *of God* are logically possible. Given a theistic understanding of God, this problem translates itself into the following problem: is it obviously inconceivable for God to bring about veridical experiences of God's self that had the property of being a veridical experience of God essentially? [18] Presupposing that it is logically possible that God exists, Oakes argues that

> there is no reason whatsoever for regarding the state of affairs consisting in a self-authenticating experience as a member of the class of states of affairs which are such that, while their description is logically possible, it is self-contradictory to claim that God brings them about. [19]

I have three objections against Oakes' last(?) effort to refute the arguments against the idea of self-authentication.

1. It could be argued that Oakes' reliance upon the analogy between propositions (having the property of being necessarily *true*) and experiences (having the property of being necessarily *veridical*) could in the last analysis prove fatal to his cause. And the reason for this is that there exists an influential and not obviously false doctrine about necessary propositions according to which such propositions—i.e. propositions the denial of which is a contradiction—are necessary because they are tautologies. Their truth is—in other words—solely dependent upon the meaning of their terms. They state nothing that is true of any particular world—they only order what we know into an intelligible whole.

If this doctrine about necessary propositions is correct, then the analogy between necessary propositions and necessarily veridical experiences would suggest that such experiences are necessarily veridical because their veridicality is solely dependent upon the current content of one's own immediate awareness. In analogy to necessary propositions, such experiences buy their peculiar property at the price of reducing their knowledge-claims about that part of reality which is not dependent upon our private awareness to zero. An example of such experiences could be experiences of one's pain or one's feelings. Such experiences do not—in themselves—imply the existence of anything independent of our mind (even if they are closely associated with "assumptions" about certain external states of affairs). Such experiences could—possibly—have the property of being necessarily veridical.

But experiences of God could not possibly have this property. Experiences of God involve claims about (e.g.) the existence of God, a claim which has ramifications which range far beyond one's own psychological state. We are brought back to our former objection against the argument of Oakes.[20]

2. Let us examine Oakes' argument for the claim that being essentially veridical and being self-authenticating are logically equivalent properties. What is inconceivable to Oakes is, namely, "that the person who hade the relevant experience should both believe (truly, of course) that it was veridical and not know that it was".[21] Let us grant Oakes the point that a person who knows that an experience has the property of being essentially veridical would not need to know anything else in order to be rationally certain that the experience is veridical. It is this which makes these experiences particularly important in an effort to defend the thesis of self-authentication. But let us now ask the following question: what must (logically) be the case, if a person were to gain knowledge that an experience is veridical through an experience being essen-

tially veridical—and through that experience alone? Well, the mere having of such an experience is, clearly, not sufficient. This is also admitted by Oakes:

> ... nothing said above should be taken to imply that it would be inconceivable for anyone who had the experience that was veridical essentially ... to believe that that experience was non-veridical; we must allow for the possibility of human irrationality even in the face of the "self-authenticating".[22]

Oakes, however, claims, that if a person *believes* that an experience is veridical *and* if the experience is essentially veridical, then such a person may also be said to have *knowledge* that the experience is veridical. In other words: belief that an experience is veridical + the having of an experience which is *essentially* veridical = knowledge that the experience is veridical.

I would argue, however, that something else has to be the case if a person were to gain knowledge that an experience is veridical without considering anything but the experience alone. True belief that an experience is veridical is not sufficient for knowledge. An experience, E, cannot be the sole foundation of a person's, A's, knowledge that E is veridical, if A does not know that E has the property of being *essentially* veridical. If the subject of the experience did not *know* that his or her experience was an experience with the property of being essentially veridical, he or she could not possibly know (in the strongest sense of the word) that the experience was veridical *on the basis of that experience alone.*

So the main question now becomes the following: how do we know that an experience has the property of being *essentially veridical?* Certainly different methods for gaining knowledge about which *propositions* have the property of being-true-necessarily have been proposed. Oakes does not, however, give us any guidance when it comes to the question of gaining knowledge of which *experiences* are essentially veridical. Until such guidance is given we have no possibility of distinguishing false claims to self-authentication from true ones.—This argument is *not* an argument against the idea of self-authenticating religious experiences. It is rather an argument against the possiblity for anyone to know which experiences are truly self-authenticating.

3. I do not think that Oakes is correct when he claims that there are "no reasons whatsoever" for the position that it is logically impossible that God brings about self-authenticating experiences of God's self. On the contrary, there are reasons to assume that this is logically impossible. If it is the case (which we have reasons to assume) that only experiences with minimal ramifications can be considered as candidates for self-authentication, then it appears that experiences of God cannot (logically) be self-authenticating. I shall not reiterate this argument.

111

There is another reason for suspecting, that the whole idea of God bringing about self-authenticating experiences of God's self is incoherent. There are influential theological systems according to which God created finite but intelligent creatures with the possibility of freely entering into or freely abstaining from a relationship with their Creator and Maker.[23] It is doubtful whether the assertion that God created men and women with this particular purpose is consistent with the claim that God also brings about self-authenticating experiences of God's self. For if God were to bring about such experiences (assuming that such experiences are possible), then it would also be the case that God would force God's creatures into a relationship with God's self.

There might, of course, be other and more cogent versions of the thesis that self-authenticating religious experiences are possible and detectable. But Oakes has not (even if he has made considerable efforts) provided us with any good reasons for thinking that such versions are forthcoming. His articles from 1972 and 1976 may meet some of the arguments directed against the idea of self-authenticating religious experiences. But the main argument against this idea—that experiences pointing beyond themselves to something independent of the experience cannot (logically) be sufficient to establish what they are pointing at—is not refuted by the arguments in these articles. Even if it should be the case that Oakes' article from 1979 justifies the claim that the idea of such experiences is coherent, Oakes has not succeeded in showing us how true claims of self-authentication could be distinguished from false ones.

External criteria

Let us now turn to the external criteria, i.e. those criteria which could be applied to religious experiences not only by those who have such experiences but also by those who receive reports from others about such experiences.

It is clear, I think, that the external criteria for judging religious experiences are far from clear and not very easy to apply. But this is not to say that there are no such criteria operative in the religious field. John Hick gives an example of one important such criterion.

> Each of the great religious traditions, including Christianity, has in fact its criteria by which to distinguish between authentic and inauthentic forms of religious experience. The most basic criterion, common to all the great traditions, is ethical, based upon observation of the moral fruits in the experiencer's life; and by this criterion almost everybody would agree that the Jim Jones type of person was either mentally or morally deranged and was desperately deluded.[24]

In this context it is, however, necessary to make a distinction between two questions. The *first* question whether the *whole* realm of religious experiences

112

is illusory. The *second* question arises if the first question is answered in the negative: how do we—*within* the realm of religious experience as a whole—distinguish between veridical and non-veridical religious experiences? Now Hick is concerned with the second question. But elsewhere he has concerned himself with the first—and more basic—question. We shall, first, turn to an assessment of his and other efforts to defend a negative answer to this question.

External arguments for the veridicality of religious experiences

Hick takes the conviction of being conscious of a physical external world, as a paradigm of a rational and adequately grounded one. We cannot in a strict sense *prove* the existence of an external world either inductively or deductively.[25] But we do not consider ourselves less justified on account of this in claiming knowledge of this external world. We are justified, according to Hick, in claiming knowledge of an external world, which transcends our immediate sensory experience because there is evidence—namely, our sensory experience—which makes our conviction about the existence of the physical external world inevitable *and* because our certitude receives further support when we act on the basis of our belief. In this respect, Hick maintains, the religious claim to have knowledge of God, is analogous to the universal claim to have knowledge of the external world. God's existence too, can neither be proved deductively or inductively. Nor is it possible, Hick says, to show that God does *not* exist. Is a religious person nevertheless justified in claiming knowledge of God? Yes, answers Hick, provided that there is evidence which makes this certitude inevitable *and* that this certitude is further supported when one acts on the basis of one's belief. Hick maintains that the great religious figures satisfy these requirements:

> The sense of the presence of God reported by the great religious figures has a similar involuntary and compelling quality; and as they proceed to live on the basis of it they are sustained and confirmed by their further experiences in the conviction that they are living in relation, not to illusion, but to reality.[26]

There are three critical questions, which one cannot avoid raising:

1. Is the faith which in Hick's sense is adequately grounded, uncoerced? That the religious interpretation of existence taken as a whole is a matter of free choice, is certainly a central idea in Hick's theory about religious faith as "experiencing-as".[27]

2. Do all religious persons embrace their belief with "inevitable certitude"? The faith of ordinary believers seems not to be combined with the same strong feeling of certitude as that of mystics and prophets. Thus according to Hick's criterion the majority of religious people are not justified in claiming knowledge of God.[28]

3. What conclusions are to be drawn from the fact that religious people are entitled in claiming incompatible knowledge about supernatural states of affair? Hick has discussed this problem in different contexts. He thinks that the incompatibility between diverging justified claims to religious knowledge (e.g. between Jews, Christians and Muslims) need not imply a problem if one presupposes that the conflict one day—i.e. in an afterlife—will be able to be resolved.[29] But the question about the conflict between different religions and how this is to be treated and resolved, is one which we must refrain from dealing with here.

Another attempt to reject the sceptical claim that *all* religious experiences are illusory is found in Richard Swinburne's book *The Existence of God*. Swinburne claims that there exists a basic principle of rationality which he calls the Principle of Credulity. Swinburne claims that according to this principle— and in the absence of special considerations—religious experiences should be accepted as evidence for the existence of God or other supernatural objects. Swinburne formulates the Principle of Credulity in the following way:

> (in the absense of special considerations) . . . if it seems (epistemically) to a subject that x is present, then probably x is present; what one seems to perceive is probably so. How things seem to be is good grounds for a belief about how things are.[30]

Swinburne's principle of credulity is certainly a principle of rationality as far as ordinary experiences concern. But is it really possible to extend the range of this principle to the field or religious experiences? This is a reasonable question, since religious experience involve a unique existence-claim, which is not involved in ordinary experiences of the world. Religious experiences involves a more or less hidden assumption that there is a dimension of reality, which transcends the physical world (as well as human minds). It is this quality which gives religious experiences their special and controversial character. And it is this quality which makes it difficult to extend the application of Swinburne's principle of credulity to the field of religious experiences without further ado.

Another possibility

I would argue that there is another way of defending the claim that the whole realm of religious experience is not an illusion. This defence is suggested by Basil Mitchell in the following quotation. Basil Mitchell is discussing Wisdom's famous parable about the invisible gardener:

> It is only in the light of some overall theory that the man in the garden could be entitled to claim that what he experienced really was (amounted to) being in the presence of and hearing the voice of the gardener . . .
> Similarly with claims to be directly aware of the presence of God. It is assumed that claims to direct awareness of God must be either self-authenticating or disguised inferences. Since they are clearly not self-authenticating they must be disguised inferences. I suggest that they are what they purport to be, cases of direct awareness, but that the claim that this is what they are relies upon there being a theory or conceptual scheme in terms of which the claim can be adequately defended.[31]

In another context Anders Jeffner has suggested what such a defence of religious experience would amount to, namely "an openness towards a specific metaphysics".[32] Such an openness would require two things: first an argument which shows that a naturalistic world-view, which makes it impossible for religious experiences to be veridical, is wrong. And secondly—and more positively—at least an outline of a metaphysics which would make it possible for at least some religious experiences to be veridical. These things will be the main issues in the next chapter of this study.

NOTES

[1] Baillie 1939, p. 143.
[2] Oakes 1979, p. 217.
[3] Mavrodes 1970, p. 79—See also Oakes 1972, p. 258.
[4] Oakes 1972, p. 262.
[5] Oakes 1972, p. 263.
[6] Hubbeling 1981, p. 60.
[7] Oakes 1976, p. 314.
[8] Oakes 1976, p. 317.
[9] Yandell 1977, p. 11.
[10] Ibid.
[11] Yandell 1977, p. 15
[12] Yandell 1977, pp. 15 f.
[13] Yandell 1977, p. 17.
[14] Oakes 1979, p. 217.
[15] Oakes 1979, p. 220 f.
[16] Oakes 1979, pp. 221 f.

[17] Oakes 1979, p. 222.
[18] Oakes 1979, p. 223.
[19] Ibid.
[20] See above pp. 107 f.
[21] Oakes 1979, pp. 222 f.
[22] Oakes 1979, p. 222.
[23] See Hick 1966, p. 135.
[24] Hick 1983, p. 36.
[25] Hick 1973, p. 110.
[26] Hick 1973, p. 112.
[27] Hick attempts to solve this problem in Hick 1973, p. 114.
[28] Mitchell 1981, p. 109.
[29] Hick 1973, p. 117–120.
[30] Swinburne 1979, p. 254.
[31] Michell 1981, pp. 114 f.
[32] Jeffner 1977, p. 82.

Chapter 9

Metaphysics and religious experience

"Metaphysics" is a difficult term—and it is associated with strong emotions in many philosophical and theological quarters. In Protestant theology, metaphysics—whatever the meaning of the term—has been judged more or less negatively. Similarly, analytical philosophers have not found much of value in metaphysical speculation. But a change in the theological and philosophical climate has occurred during recent years. This is not—needless to say—any argument for the rationality of metaphysics. But it provides us with a welcome opportunity to explore the relationship between this kind of thinking and religious experience.

In this chapter I shall not enter into a detailed elaboration and defence of metaphysics as a rational philosophical subject. This has been done by other scholars who can be considered as contemporary specialists in this particular field.[1] In the present context I shall content myself with giving rough outline of a metaphysical world-view. Such a world-view can be characterized as an overall framework of reality. Metaphysical thinking is the search for the ultimate structures of reality, by which it is possible to comprehend empirical reality as a whole. Metaphysical world-views cannot—in contrast to limited hypotheses about particular events within empirical reality—be subjected to falsification by a test-case. Nevertheless, they can be both true and important. They reflect a deep propensity of the human mind: the quest for intelligibility.[2] (Needless to say, the term "metaphysics" is also used for other purposes. Still it is not uncommon to use the term in the way we do in the present context.)

In the following I shall introduce the concept of explanatory system. The sciences provide us with different explanatory systems. Metaphysical systems can be described as explanatory systems—not for a specific area of reality but for empirical reality as a whole. Metaphysical systems are sometimes modelled after explanatory models in the sciences. Certain metaphysical system use causal explanations as their main model and seek "the Ground of Being". Other metaphysical systems proceed from the teleological model of explanation and start with some idea about the ends or purposes for which the empirical world exists. In Plato's doctrine of ideas we find a curious blending of these two models of explanation. The ideas exist as the Grounds of Being—but they are also the ideals to which the things of this world are directed.

I would argue that both kinds of metaphysics—a cosmological metaphysics of the "Ground" as well as a teleological metaphysics of the "Purpose"—are required to give an adequate view of reality as a whole. Being calls for some idea about the ground—or grounds—of being. And the phenomenon of time calls for some idea about the future (immanent or transcendent) to which our present activities should be directed. In the following I shall give a further reason for the necessity of teleological metaphysics. But in the main part of this chapter, I shall, however, limit myself to saying a few words about the first type of metaphysics (cosmological metaphysics), about why I think such a metaphysics cannot dispense with the idea of the transcendent and about the relevance of such a metaphysics for our epistemological attitude towards religious experience.

Explanatory systems

To begin with, we shall introduce the concept of explanatory systems. This concept has been suggested in a different context by Anders Jeffner.[3] An explanatory system is a connected set of theories and methods by means of which we can get answers to such questions as why something is the case or why something ought to be the case. Physics is one explanatory system and a moral theory such as utilitarianism is another. A theology such as the one developed by Thomas Aquinas can also be regarded as an explanatory system. There are also theories of action which can be regarded as explanatory systems especially designed for the explanation of human actions.[4]

Now a central problem concerning explanatory systems is the following: which explanatory systems are sufficient for an adequate explanation of empirical reality? Clearly, this question requires some *criteria of adequacy*. We shall formulate two: a set of explanatory system is sufficient for an adequate explanation of empirical reality if and only if (1) the set of systems does not leave any parts of empirical reality unexplained, disorted or "explained away" and (2) among the set of explanatory systems there must be one explanatory system the explanatory factors of which do not themselves require any further explanation.

The first of these two criteria of adequacy seems quite evident. If there are parts of reality left unexplained, then it does not seem reasonable to say that the set of explanatory systems is sufficient for an adequate explanation of reality. But the second criterion of adequacy might seem more difficult to understand. What kind of explanatory factors are those which do not themselves require any further explanation? We shall return to this question below: at this stage it is sufficient to say that it is nothing strange with the idea of factors not requiring any further explanation. It might be the case that there is no further explanation or that these factors are self-explanatory. And, surely, an *adequate* explanation of empirical reality must provide us with an explanatory system the factors of which either do not have any further explanation or are self-explanatory.

Then some words about the concept of explanation. What does it mean to give an explanation of something? We must observe that the need for an explanation arises in confrontation with puzzling phenomena. According to John Hick—"to explain a puzzling phenomenon is to set it in a wider context, or in connection with some further circumstance, in which it is no longer puzzling."[5] Different kinds of explanations can also be distinguished from the perspective of the kind of context which is considered to explain a puzzling phenomenon. Following Richard Swinburne, we might distinguish between scientific explanations and personal explanations. A scientific explanation involves explaining a particular phenomenon by viewing it as an instance of a general law.[6] A personal explanation occurs when a puzzling phenomenon—most notably human actions—is set in connection with the motives and intentions of a person.[7] (The relationship between scientific and personal explanations is a matter of considerable controversy and we shall return to this problem below.) Scientific and personal explanations could in turn be distinguished from normative explanations, where a human action is judged with reference to a principle which prescribes that certain actions ought to be done.

Let us now return to the particular question formulated above: which explanatory systems are sufficient for an adequate explanation of empirical reality? One particular answer presents itself naturally in our context of a scientific and technological culture: physics and chemistry provide us with those sorts of explanatory systems which are sufficient for an adequate explanation of reality. It would be clearly misleading to characterize this answer with the word "materialism". The claim that physics and chemistry provide us with the sorts of explanatory systems which are sufficient for an adequate explanation of reality is not incompatible with the claim that there exists many things besides material objects, i.e. "modes of action, relations of meaning, dreams, joys, plans, aspirations".[8] It is one thing to claim that propositions dealing with, for example, mental events are *logically deducible* from propositions dealing exclusively with physical ones. It is another thing to argue that mental phenomena are sufficiently *explained* in the explanatory system of physics and chemistry.[9] This is an instance of the larger claim that physics and chemistry are sufficient for a explanation of every aspect of reality. We might label it "naturalism". The best statement of this philosophy is found in Ernest Nagel's book *Logic without Metaphysics* (publ. 1956) and, more particularly, in its first chapter entitled "Naturalism reconsidered".

Nagel does not present his view as an exposition of the claim that physics and chemistry provide us with the sorts of explanatory systems which are sufficient for an adequate explanation of reality. But I think that his naturalistic philosophy without distortion can be understood in these terms.

Two theses of naturalism

Nagel summarizes his particular version of naturalism in two theses. In the first thesis he claims that naturalism fulfils our first criterion of adequacy in the second that it fulfils our second criterion.

a) *Nagel's first thesis*

In his first thesis Nagel argues "the existential and causal primacy of organized matter in the executive order of nature". Nagel explains this claim in the following way:

> This is the assumption that the occurrence of events, qualities and processes, and the characteristic behaviours of various individuals, are contingent upon the organization of spatio-temporally located bodies, whose internal structures and external relations determine and limit the appearance and disappearance of everything that happens.[10]

Nagel further claims that this is "one of the best-tested conclusions of experience". But to assess this justification of the first thesis of naturalism, we must first come to grips with the thesis itself. I would argue that what the thesis amounts to is that the explanatory systems of physics and chemistry do not leave any parts of empirical reality unexplained. But once the essence of the first thesis of naturalism is brought forth accordingly, its truth does no longer appear as obvious. There are certain parts of reality which do not readily let themselves to an explanation in the explanatory systems of physics and chemistry. Let me give five examples.

Let us, first, consider biological phenomena. It is the case that biological phenomena can be explained in the explanatory systems of physics and chemistry? A positive answer to this question would imply—as Carl Hempel has argued—that all aspects of the behaviour of living organisms can be explained by means of physico-chemical laws and theories. As Hempel has pointed out the truth of this claim cannot be established by *a priori* argument; it must be decided by biological and biophysical research. For all we know, it *could* be the case that the laws and principles of the explanatory system of biology are explained in the explanatory systems of physics and chemistry. This would require a unifying theory with bridge principles connecting biological laws with physico-chemical laws in such a way that the operation of a physico-chemical

120

law is a necessary and sufficient condition for the operation of a biological law. But such a unifying theory has not yet been constructed, let alone empirically tested. Nothing prevents the scientist from entertaining such a unified theory "as a principle for the guidance of research".[11] But it is clearly premature to entertain such a unified theory as an established fact. Yet this is precisely what the naturalist asks us to do—no less than a "sacrificium intellectu" where we certainly would not expect it.

Consider further mental phenomena. Is it the case that mental phenomena can be explained in the explanatory system of physics and chemistry (or perhaps biology)? This would imply that certain physico-chemical laws or biological laws could be explain the regularities of mental life. This would also require the introduction of a set of bridge principles or—in this case—psycho-physical laws. Needless to say, we are far from having such a theory which unifies physics and psychology. Some philosophers have even argued that it is impossible in principle to formulate such a theory. Donald Davidson has argued that because of the "holistic character of the cognitive field" there are no psycho-physical laws. In addition he says:

> An effort at increasing the accuracy and power of a theory of behaviour forces us to bring more and more of the whole system of the agent's beliefs and motives directly into account. But in inferring this system from the evidence, we necessarily impose conditions of coherence, rationality, and consistency. These conditions have no echo in physical theory, which is why we can look for no more than rough correlations between psychological and physical phenomena.[12]

There are further problems for the naturalist when we bring experiences of freedom and identity into play. These experiences suggest that human beings are autonomous agents. This is clearly contrary to the affirmation of the naturalist that everything can be explained in the explanatory system of physics and chemistry. The obvious move for the naturalist is to argue that these experiences are illusory—we may experience freedom and autonomy but these experiences cannot be trusted as veridical. The alternative is to take these significant experiences seriously and construe an explanatory system of a personalistic character in which those human actions can be explained which cannot readily be explained in the explanatory system of physics and chemistry. Needless to say, difficult conflicts could arise in certain instances—or perhaps in a greater set of situations—concerning which explanatory system (i.e. the personalistic or the physico-chemical one) should be applied. Consider the simple situation of a man raising his hand. There are clearly situations in which it could be difficult to decide whether this action should be explained in a physico-chemical explanatory system (as a reflex) or in a personalistic explanatory system (as an intended sign with a certain meaning).

There is further the problem caused by the occurrence of moral experiences, i.e. experiences of what Stuart Hampshire call "morally impossible actions" and the intrinsic goodness of certain things, for example, the sancity of human life. Nagel affirms that "men are animated by many springs of action, no one of which is intrinsically good or evil; and a moral ideal is the imagined satisfaction of some complex of impulses, desires and needs".[13] But that there are some things that are intrinsically good—such as the integrity of human persons—and that there are certain things that are "categorically excluded and forbidden morally"—such as torturing human persons—does seem to belong to our very concept of morality. Naturalism asks us to take leave of us this concept, but it is not at all clear that naturalism itself is sufficiently established to legitimate such a demand.

Lastly, there are of course experiences of transcendence. These experiences cannot be veridical for a naturalist since everything is ultimately dependant upon physico-chemical laws and particulars. But experiences of transcendence suggest that reality is "spatio-temporal and more".[14] As I have argued earlier it is not sufficient for the naturalist to argue that experiences of transcendence are illusory because they are amenable to an explanation in—let us say—the explanatory system of physics and chemistry. The philosophical theologian could always argue that these experiences are over-determined by the presence of a transcendent reality. The existence of such a reality is denied by the naturalist—and this claim is based upon his or her conviction that reality is spatio-temporal and *no* more. We shall shortly return to this impasse between the believer and the naturalist—and ask ourselves, whether there is any way to decide who is right.

b) *Nagel's second thesis*

Let us now proceed to consider another important element of naturalism. Nagel formulates it in the form of his second thesis:

> The second major contention of naturalism is that the manifest plurality and variety of things, of their qualities and their functions, are an irreducible feature of the cosmos, not a deceptive appearance cloaking some more homogenous "ultimate reality" or transempirical substance, and that the sequential orders in which events occur or the manifold relations of dependence in which things exist are *contingent* connections, not the embodiments of a fixed and unified pattern of logically necessary links.[15]

I understand the essence of this thesis as a claim that the explanatory system of physics and chemistry fulfils the second criterion of adequacy, i.e. that the basic factors in the physico-chemical explanatory system—matter (as it is constituted by molecules, atoms, subatomic particles, quarks, subquarks etc.) and the laws govering the movement of matter—are such that they do not require any further explanation. This claim is *not* inconsistent with the fact that creative conceptformation *within* the explanatory scheme of physics and chemistry has taken place and will take place. Different kinds of explanatory levels *within* the physico-chemical explanatory system are continually being discerned. The recent development concerning quarks can be seen in this perspective.

What is denied, however, is that there exists another explanatory scheme altogether which is more basic than the physico-chemical explanatory system—in the sense of a condition for the existence of the basic factors of the physico-chemical explanatory system, i.e. matter and laws. Explanations in terms of the qualities of material particulars and the laws that govern their relationships do not require any further explanation in terms of the trans-empirical. Naturalism affirms *the ultimate character of the physico-chemical explanatory system.*

Why should we believe that this affirmation is true? Nagel is not very clear upon this point. He does not make any reference—as would be expected—to the principle of parsimony (or Occam's razor): a simpler explanation—an explanation which assumes fewer principles of explanation—is to be preferred to a more complicated one. This is, needless to say, a strong argument in favour of naturalism. The force of this argument can, however, be somewhat diminished, if we consider the integration of our world-view which could result from the introduction of a metaphysical explanatory system. I say "could" because it is obvious that not every metaphysical explanatory system which has been proposed, results in what could be called "an integration of our world-view".

But even if it is hard to discern any clear arguments for the priority of the physico-chemical explanatory system, there are, however, more particular arguments against a Hegelian type of metaphysics, which affirms that "whatever occurs is a phase in a unitary, teleologically organized, and all-inclusive process or system".[16] The main objection against such a metaphysical explanatory system is that by affirming that the universe embodies "a fixed and unified pattern of logically links" it does not do justice to the fact that most processes in the universe are causally irrelevant to each other and that everything (or at least some things) is contingent.

The existence of causal irrelevance and contingency in the universe is clearly a reason against certain forms of metaphysical explanatory systems. But this does not imply that the idea of a metaphysical explanatory system as a whole is untenable.

The possibility of a metaphysical explanatory system

So far we have only considered two important arguments for the ultimate character of the physico-chemical explanatory system. We may call them the argument from parsimony and the argument from the untenability of the alternatives. We have argued that these arguments are not decisive. Let us now consider an argument against the claim that the physico-chemical explanatory scheme has an ultimate character.

It goes without saying that we live in a complex universe. Consider the physical and biological processes with which we are confronted in our everyday life. Consider the interaction between human beings and groups of human beings during history. And consider the vast universe with its diversity and multitude of galaxies, stars and planets.[17] *If* the first thesis of naturalism is true and everything can be explained in the explanatory system of physics and chemistry, then a considerable simplification of our world-view would occur. Let us—for the sake of the argument—assume that this is possible. Let us also assume that many of the present complexities of the physico-chemical explanatory system could be removed. Thus, somewhere in the furture the human race may arrive at a unified and extremely simple theory of nature. Yet, it could be argued that there exists a duality which cannot be eliminated even in such a theory, namely the duality between material particulars ("facts") and laws (which describe the relationships between material particulars). To reduce statement of laws to statements about material particulars would end in failure because particular existents cannot be manufactured out of mere universals. And the attempt to reduce statements about material particulars to statements about laws is impossible for another reason, which has been well formulated by Alfred Taylor:

> The more we advance to the reduction of the visible face of Nature to "law", the more, not the less, complex and baffling become the mass of characters which we have to attribute as bare unexplained fact to our ultimate constituents. An electron is a much stiffer does of "brute" fact than one of Newton's hard impenetrable corpuscles.[18]

Thus, we have a duality between "facts" and "laws" which cannot be eliminated from science *even if we presuppose that a unified and extremely simply theory is forthcoming somewhere in the future.* We have found reason to question this presupposition. Thus, there might be not only a duality between law and fact, but also between matter and life, body and mind, mind and the mind's I, "is" and "ought". The objective need for a metaphysical explanatory system arises when we confront ourselves with this pluralism. The natural attitude towards this pluralism of one or more dualities would seem to be to not content ourselves—as Bertrand Russell did in his famous discussion with Frederick Copleston—that "it's just there!" This would imply—as Alfred Taylor said—that we put "unintelligible mystery at the very heart of reality" and that we denied "the very assumption on which science is built".[19] And if the introduction of a metaphysical reality could relieve us of the embarrassment caused by the dualities of the empirical universe, then this must be counted as an argument in favour of the existence of such a reality.

The naturalist affirms that the explanatory system of physics and chemistry is sufficient for an adequate explanation of empirical reality. I have argued that this is false and that a metaphysical explanatory system is—ultimately—required to give an adequate explanation of the empirical reality as a whole. But it must be clearly admitted that my argument does not amount to a conclusive proof. But neither do the arguments of the naturalist. Thus, we are not in a position to make a decision which can be shown to be fully rational. There are, to be sure, arguments in the field, but not of a kind which once and for all settles the matter. Naturalism and nonnaturalism are large-scale interpretations of a wide range of facts, theories and experiences. We should not be surprised to find that matters in this field are not easily settled by objective argumentation. I have tried to give some reasons why I find a nonnaturalistic interpretation more convincing than a naturalistic one. But these reasons do not amount to a conclusive proof.

When we introduced an ultimate reality beyond the physical world, then the arguments for the introduction of such a new ontological category should not be confused with the type of argument relevant for the existence of entities within an ontological category (here lies the mistake in all effort to "locate" the soul). The ultimate reality of a metaphysical explanatory system is another kind of being, not just another member of a class of finite objects.[20]

There are—at least—three things which we have reason to expect from a metaphysical system which transcends the bounds of our ordinary empirical reality. We should expect that such an explanatory system introduces a new ontological category (and not just another thing) which a) has the property of ontological independence, i.e. that the purported reality does not depend upon anything else for its existence[21], b) is the universal ground for the existence of everything else in the universe, i.e. if the ultimate reality did not exist, then nothing would exist, c) makes allowance for the contingencies and necessities in all dimensions (physical, biological, psychological, social, religious etc.) of reality in a way that preserves their irreducible properties.

If we impose these conditions upon our conception of ultimate reality, then the Judeo-Christian concept of Deity lies close at hand. It is, namely, possible to affirm that God is the universal ground of being *without at the same denying the contingency of (i.e. the non-deterministic character of) human action.* The possibility of such a religious metaphysics was gratuitously excluded by Nagel. But this alternative has been elaborated by Wolfhart Pannenberg in an important article from 1959. He explains how God (as God is understood in the Judeo-Christian tradition) can be the universal ground without denying the contingencies nor the necessities of human history:

> Der Gott, der durch die Transzendenz seiner Freiheit Ursprung des Kontingenten in der Welt ist, begründet auch die Einheit des Kontingenten als Geschichte so, dass die Kontingenz der in ihr verbundenen Ereignisse nicht ausgeschlossen wird. Nur der Ursprung der Kontingenz der Geschehnisse kann, so scheint es, vermöge seiner Einheit auch Ursprung ihres Zusammenhanges sein, ohne ihre Kontingenz zu beeinträchtigen. Die Einheit der Ereignisse besteht nun aber nicht nur in ihrem transzendenten Ursprung, sondern hängen auch untererinander zusammen. Dieser dem Geschehen innewohnende Zusammenhang gründet in der ihm transzendenten Einheit Gottes, der sich als Treue manifestiert.[21b]

Theism also affirms that God has many other properties besides the property of being the ultimate reality. Any analysis of such a claim would require an extensive analysis, which cannot be performed in the present context. But the most that can be done here is to give some brief suggestions why it seems more reasonable than not to affirm that ultimate reality is *transcendent, personal* and *worthy of worship.*

Transcendence.—If we affirm the existence of a reality beyond the factors referred to in the physico-chemical explanatory scheme, then it does not seem reasonable to assume that the "truly" ultimate reality is *within* space and time. And the reason for this is that space and time are closely entwined with the material reality. The developments in physics have shown us that space cannot be taken as some kind of cosmic "container" filled with material particulars. Neither is it possible to define many of the central properties of matter without reference to time. This suggests that a metaphysical explanatory system is necessary to account for space and time as well as matter and its laws.

It must, however, be observed that this concept of transcendence creates certain problems for such a central affirmation of the Christian faith as the idea of divine acitivity in the world. Activity seems to imply immanence.[22] We shall not enter into a discussion of these problems in the present context. It is sufficient to note the reluctance of Christian theologians to solve this conflict by giving up the idea of transcendence altogether.

Personality.—The idea of personality is closely connected with the idea of autonomy. A person is a being whose actions are not (at least not exclusively) determined by external factors. A person is in an important sense free. Now, we may derive one reason for the propensity to understand the "truly" ultimate in personal terms from the fact that it is ontologically independent. Thereby it would seem to exemplify the idea of a person in an expressive way. But this does not seem sufficient to justify a personal conception of the "truly" ultimate. The idea of a person is also linked to such concepts as intentions and purposes. One important question is, then, the following: does the universe as a whole—or in parts—express signs of a purposive activity which cannot be explained with reference to human or other immanent persons? But for an answer to this question we are forced into the area of teleological metaphysics. Before we say a few words about this, let us consider another central property of Deity.

Worthy of worship, praise and thanksgiving.—If God is the universal ground of being, is it then possible that God is also worthy of praise, worship and thanksgiving? The presence of evil in the world seems to exclude this possibility. If God is the universal ground of being, then God is also the ground of all evil and suffering in the world. And if this is the case, then (it is often said) God cannot be worthy of praise and worship, because a God which sustains so much evil and suffering cannot be wholly good (which God must be to be worthy of praise and worship).

Vincent Brümmer has, however, argued that it is appropriate for a person to give thanks to another person for a good thing this latter person has done even if he or she—unintentionally, of course—at the same time brought about an unavoidable evil. Similarly, we give thanks only for those good things which God brings about intentionally—and not for those evil things which God necessarily brings about unintentionally. Vincent Brümmer says that "we thank him for events in which he realizes his purposes, and not for events which he permits even though they are contrary to his will".[23]

The most obvious object of thanksgiving for a Christian is God's creation of the world. Thanking God for God's creation of the world presupposes at least four different things: *first,* some over-all idea about the good purpose for which God creates the world. Teilhard de Chardin has given a contemporary outline of such a teleological metaphysics. As human consciousness has arisen out of physical matter, so will also a great communion of love—the realm of God—arise out of the human community.[24] Teilhard argued that such a teleological interpretation of the world need not make us acquiesce in things as they happen, but can urge us to actions whose end has been set not by finite creatures but by the will of God.[25] *Secondly,* thanksgiving for God's creation of the world presupposes that the purpose for which God creates the world necessarily requires an area of evil, suffering and chaos in the world. Such an area is, then, unavoidably and unintentionally sustained by God in that God creates a world with the purpose of realizing community and love. For example: it is a necessary condition for mutual experience of community between human beings and God that the moral and religious attitudes of human beings are not determined by God.[26] If God creates a universe for the purpose of community, God cannot at the same time determine the moral and religious attitudes of human beings. But if God does bring about that their moral and religious attitudes are not determined by God, then God has to sustain human beings misusing their freedom in evil deeds, as well as a cognitive distance between God and humankind. A "veil"—like the evolving physical universe—is required. Only an evolving physical universe with stable laws can allow for a religious as well as a non-religious interpretation. But such a universe must include an area of chaos and suffering. Brian Hebblethwaite says: "Only a flexible organism evolving from a host of mutually interacting systems, combining law-governed processes with genuine spontaneity, can be the vehicle of finite free and personal life and thought. But such a process and such creatures are bound to be at risk to accidental clashes, at different levels of created being—atomic, molecular, organic and so on. Nevertheless, it is in some such process as this which is the necessary condition of finite personal being."[27]

Thirdly, thankgiving to God for creating the world presupposes that it is a better thing to create the world with the purpose God creates it (and with the evil and suffering this necessarily requires) than to create no world at all. It is not, however, evident that this condition is fulfiled. Dostoevsky even affirmed that the suffering of one tiny creature is sufficient to tip the balance in favour of no world at all:

> Imagine that you are creating a fabric of human destiny with the object of making men happy in the end, giving them peace and rest at last, but that it was essential and inevitable to torture to death only one tiny creature and to found that edifice on its unavenged tears, would you consent to be the architect on these conditions? Tell me, and tell me the truth![28]

It is, surely, preposterous to claim that the happiness of other human beings could compensate the suffering of others. It is, however, another thing if the person permitting the suffering is capable of compensating the victim fully for his or her suffering. George Schlesinger has explained what this could mean:

> By 'fully compensate' I mean that the victim will eventually agree that the experience of suffering which A had subjected him to in the pursuit of his stated goal, together with the subsequent compensation, is no less preferable to having had neither experience. It is obvious that only God is in the position to be able to guarantee this.[29]

Similarly, John Hick argues that "the Christian answer must be in terms of a future good great enough to justify all that has happened on the way to it."[30]

But, *fourthly*, thankgiving to God for creating the world also presupposes not only the idea of God fully compensating all the victims of evil and suffering in the world, but also that this idea is not merely a claim *ad hoc,* i.e. a claim which is made *solely* for the purpose of rescuing the Christian attitude of praise, worship and thanksgiving towards God.[31]

These points have served the purpose of defending the claim that the ultimate reality of our metaphysical explanatory system and the concept of God (in theism) can be identified without significant distortion. But this hypothesis needs further corroboration; my intention has merely been to show how metaphysical reflection might get started—its detailed development is another thing.

Religious experience in the light of metaphysics

Let us now close this chapter by some reflections upon the relevance of a metaphysics (of the character outlined in the former part of this chapter) for the assessment of religious experiences. I perceive three areas of relevance:

1. If we are justified in adopting the kind of metaphysical explanatory system, which we have outlined above, then we have an independent argument for the existence of an object which at least a large class of religious experiences claim. It might be the case—as we assumed in chapter 7—that these experiences are sufficiently conditioned by natural factors of a physiological, psychological or sociological nature. If the arguments of natural theology are tenable, then the assumption that these experiences are over-determined by a transempirical reality cannot simply be discarded as *ad hoc*-assumptions, i.e. assumptions developed with no other intention than to save the veridical character of those experiences. In other words: in the light of our metaphysical explanatory system, religious experiences may have a natural explanation even if they at the same time are conditioned by a transempirical reality.

2. Our metaphysical explanatory system might also provide us with a set of criteria with the help of which, we might be able to distinquish genuine religious experiences from non-genuine ones. Such criteria might become available through the character of the metaphysical system itself and, more precisely, through the properties of the ultimate reality the existence of which our metaphysical explanatory system gives us reason to assume. We have reason to reject crude materialistic experiences of ultimate reality as illusory and accept experiences of a transcendent ground of being as veridical. Other

types of criteria for distinguishing genuine religious experiences will be discussed in the final chapter of this study.

3. Our metaphysical explanatory system might also deepen our insight into the nature of religious experiences. Most religious experiences are at the same time experiences of something else in this empirical world. Take the following example. When David Livingstone asked a tswana-man in Africa about his conception of holiness (boitsepho) he received the following answer:

> When heavy showers have fallen during the night and when earth, leaves and cattle are washed clean and the rising sun shows a drop of dew on every straw of grass and when the air brethes freshness—this is holiness.[32]

This moving answer can of course be interpreted in many different ways. But it clearly shows how entwined religious experiences are with experiences of *this* world. In light of the metaphysical explanatory system which we have been discussing in this chapter, such religious experiences can be understood as experiences of a physical situation and—indirectly—of the transempirical reality upon which this physical situation (as everything else in the empirical world) is dependent as a condition of their existence.[33] The subject of the experience perceives the transempirical ground of the object of the experiences. Similarly, it might also be possible to have experiences in which the subject of the experience perceives the transempirical ground of *the experience itself* and even the ground of *the personal "I"* who is having the experience. We may recall the claims of the mystics that to find oneself, is to find God. In other words: it is possible to clarify religious experiences and their character in the light of the metaphysical explanatory system upon which we have focused in the present chapter.

In chapter 5 we argued against a simplistic view where religious experiences were taken as the verifying ground of religious beliefs. Still, we suggested that there are reasons for retaining a modified version of the hypothetical view of religious belief. In view of the words above, we may say that religious experiences cannot simply be taken as verifying instances of a religious belief. But they may nevertheless strengthen and justify the introduction of a metaphysical explanatory system by being amenable to clarification and deepened understanding with the help of the basic concepts of this explanatory system.

NOTES

[1] See Hamlyn 1984, Körner 1984 and Schlesinger 1983.

[2] See Ward 1982, pp. 4 f. Note Ward's reference to Popper and his defence of metaphysics in *The Logic of Scientific Discovery*, p. 438.

[3] See Jeffner 1977 b, p. 38.

[4] For a comprehensive analysis of such theories of human action, see Nordenfelt 1974, chapter 1.

[5] Hick 1974, p. 48.

[6] See Swinburne 1979, chapter 2.

[7] Ibid.

[8] Nagel 1956, p. 7.

[9] Nagel 1956, pp. 24 ff.

[10] Nagel 1956, p. 7.

[11] Hempel 1966, pp. 104 ff.

[12] Davidson 1976, p. 103. If Davidson is correct, then it is in principle impossible to find a scientific explanation of religious experiences. See below chapter 7.

[13] Nagel 1956, p. 11.

[14] See chapter 9, note 20.

[15] Nagel 1956, pp. 7 ff.

[16] Nagel 1956, p. 8.

[17] See Swinburne 1979, p. 130.

[18] Taylor 1970, pp. 72 f.

[19] Taylor 1970, p. 74.

[19] Taylor 1970, p. 74.

[20] See further chapter 3, pp.

[21] See further on the idea of ontological independence in Swinburne 1979, p. 48.

[21b] Pannenberg 1967, pp. 73 ff.

[22] See Pike 1970, chapter 7.

[23] Brümmer 1984, p. 95. See also Hebblethwaite 1976, pp. 72 f.

[24] See Teilhard de Chardin 1975, part III.

[25] See Singleton, p. 236.

[26] See further comments on this idea in Görman 1977, pp. 117–121, particularly p. 119.

[27] See Hebblethwaite 1976, p. 78.—Chapter 5 as a whole is valuable for understanding the context of the argument.

[28] Dostoevsky 1945, book 5, chapter 4.

[29] Schlesinger 1983, p. 66.

[30] Hick 1973, p. 43.

[31] Hick 1964, pp. 259 f.

[32] Pettersson 1966, p. 61.

[33] See further on this conception of religious experience in Mavrodes 1972, pp. 68 ff. and Oakes 1981.

Chapter 10

Our ability "to distinguish the spirits"

If we accept that it is reasonable to affirm a metaphysical explanatory system of the type we have discussed in the foregoing chapter, then the epistemological value of religious experiences increases. They can no longer be lightly classified as illusions. On the contrary, it is natural to interpret at least some of them as experiences of something real, i.e. not something which is real in the empirical world, but rather something real in the transempirical dimension of reality.

But even if a step into metaphysics might give us an answer to the first question above on pp. 112–113, the second question still remains unanswered: how do we—within the realm of religious experience as a whole—distinguish between veridical and non-veridical religious experiences? It is clearly impossible to accept *every* religious experience as veridical. But by what criterion—or criteria—do we decide which experience is veridical and which not?

Before we take a closer look at some answers to this question, one thing must be said about these answers in general. It must be clearly noticed that these "criteria of veridicality" should be regarded as starting-points for the epistemological assessment of religious experiences and not as unquestionable principles of human knowledge. Many of the terms contained in these criteria are vague and the application of these criteria calls for a judgement which is sensitive to the elusive character of religious experiences. We should not expect that any criteria can play the same rôle as—for example—epistemological principles in natural science. Basil Mitchell once wrote in connection with a discussion about the sense of "the holy" that it is neither a necessary nor a sufficient criterion of divine presence, but it is nevertheless *characteristic* of it.[1] I think that these words of Mitchell express the preliminary character of criteria in religious experience and should be in the background of the whole discussion in this chapter. We shall now consider some of the most obvious candidates for the rôle of "criteria of veridicality" in the field of religious experiences.

An empirical criterion

The first criterion has to do with the relationship between empirical facts and laws on the one hand and religious experiences on the other. It is most naturally formulated in a negative way: if a religious experience contradicts well-established empirical facts or laws, then it cannot—as a rule—be taken as veridical.

I think that some principle of this character is of value in the assessment of religious experiences. Still, we must consider some critical questions in connection with it. The anchorage of the criterion is—I think—a judgement that religious experiences cannot be admitted with the same certainty as well-established empirical facts and laws. Therefore, empirical facts and laws can serve as an instance of assessment for religious experiences. In general, I think, this is true. But it does not (as we shall see below) imply that judgement about what particular facts and laws are well-established is wholly independent of the overall world-view which a certain person accepts.

Further, some would argue that such a kind of empirical criterion is of little or no value, because (as C.D. Broad once said) "the assertions in which religious mystics agree are not such that they conflict with what we can perceive with our senses".[2] On the other hand, a conflict might occur (Broad admits) because of the mystic who affirms the unreality of matter, time and change. Such an affirmation runs counter to our most basic convictions. But it is not necessary that this conflict is irreconcilable.[3]

An obvious problem emerges when we move into the broader field of non-mystical religious experiences. It seems that religious experiences of miracles must be regarded as illusory according to the present criterion. This is a complex problem which cannot be adequately handled in the present context. I shall restrict myself to some short comments.

John Hick has underlined that "miracle" can be defined *either* in purely religious terms *or* in mixed religious and scientific terms. Hick says:

> The purely religious concept denotes events which are experienced as having powerful religious meaning, events through which individuals and communities are vividly conscious of God, and which express to them the divine goodness or love or judgement. But when miracle is defined as a mixed religious and scientific concept the proviso is added that the events in question must be contra-natural, in the sense of being incapable of natural explanation. A miracle is then regarded as an event which could not have happened unless God, in his omnipotence, had intervened in the process of the universe to cause it to happen.[4]

If we define "miracle" in the first way—as a religious concept—then religious experiences of miracles cannot conflict with the empirical criterion. But if we define it in the second way, we have a problem. Some theologicans have solved this problem by rejecting the empirical criterion altogether. This is—to say the least—an overreaction. Others—such as Hick himself—have claimed that "the more intelligible alternative is that God does not make miraculous interventions, in the sense of divine suspensions of natural law".[5] This solution seems to me to be inadequate. It is certainly the case that (1) many particular miracle-stories are false and (2) some of those miracle-stories which are true describe events which are amenable to natural explanations. But there still seems to remain a certain group of events—for example, in the life and death of Jesus Christ—where we may have some other reasons than those events themselves for believing in the unique presence of the transcendent.[6] This means that known laws cannot be applied without qualification to these events. If we have some independent reason for believing that "God was in Christ", then (as Jeffner has written in an analysis of Butler's theology) "an entirely new factor is present, and also the events that appear to follow the known laws must be excepted from their field of application. We thus have no standards by which to judge what it is probable will happen around Christ, and when we are to decide what really happened then there is nothing for us to do but to judge the credibility of the historical witnesses . . ."[7]

It is therefore wise to use the empirical criterion with some caution. But this does not imply that it is without importance. It can still be applied to those experiences which are judged to be experiences of miracles (in Hick's second sense) but which fall under natural laws (i.e. where there is no reason to assume that the events must be excepted from the field of application of known laws). Such religious experiences are non-veridical.

It should further be noticed before we leave the empirical criterion that some thinkers have employed a more positive empirical criterion and argued that religious experiences are veridical, when they are confirmed by well-established empirical facts or laws. This problem is connected with the much wider problem of religion and science. It has been misused in many quarters (for example, by Frithiof Capra). We must be aware of the fact that the whole idea of empirical facts as confirming religious experiences is open to serious philosophical and theological objections.[8]

The moral criterion

In judging religious experience, many people make use of a moral criterion. Religious experiences are judged by their fruits or by their moral content. I think that such a criterion is indispensable in the present context. But it is not easy to assess the status of this criterion—or rather set of criteria. This has to do with problems of normative ethics as well as meta-ethics. Hence a discussion about the moral criteria in religious experience would require a more extensive discussion on the meaning and justification of moral statements. In the present context, I shall hypothetically assume that it makes sense to say that moral convictions are true or false, that there are good reasons for regarding certain moral convictions as true and others as false and that logical rules apply in the moral discourse. Let us call this hypothetically assumed position "the objective view".[9]

Let us now consider four different ways in which morality might enter into the assessment of religious experiences.

Argument 1:—It is often argued that there is an important relationship between religious experience and ethical behaviour. This is often stated in the form of a negative criterion of veridicality: religious experience must be rejected as illusory if their consequences are bad (especially for those who have these experiences). It is possible to view the misgivings many persons have about mystical experiences in the light of such a moral criterion. For example: it is often said that mystical experiences cause people to withdraw from the world. Political and moral activity becomes unimportant to the person who has found his or her unity with God. Ernst Troeltsch and Max Weber have created this image of mysticism. For example, Max Weber has the following to say about mystical contemplation:

> Die Kontemplation . . . ist primär das Suchen eines 'Ruhens' im Göttlichem und nur in Ihm. Nichthandeln, in der letzter Konsequens Nichtdenken, Entleerung von Allem, was irgendwie an die 'Welt' erinnert, jedenfalls absolutes Minimisieren alles äusseren und inneren Tuns sind der Weg, denjenigen inneren Zustand zu erreichen, der als Besitz des Göttlichen, als unio mystica mit ihm, genossen wird: einen spezifischen Gefühlshabitus also, der ein 'Wissen' zu vermitteln scheint.[10]

This idea of mysticism has fostered a negative evaluation of mysticism within contemporary Protestant theology from Albert Ritschl to Karl Barth.[11] This negative evaluation presupposes 1) that a certain class of religious experiences, i.e. mystical experiences, are associated with an amoral passivity and 2) that 1) is a reason for rejecting the knowledge-claims of the mystic. But both these suppositions stand in need of further scrutiny.

When it comes to the first supposition certain results and reflections presented by Robert Wuthnow are highly relevant. In an empirical study in California 1978 Wuthnow found a positive correlation between mystical attitudes and political activity. This seems to contradict the general Weberian idea of mysticism. Wuthnow suggested in a later book an alternative idea of mysticism as morally and politically ambigous and argued that this ambiguity of mysticism is dependent upon factors in the larger social context, i.e. "the availability or unavailability of political channels, and the degree of institutional differentiation".[12] By combining high and low values on these varibles, Wuthnow distinguished between four types of societies. Wuthnow claims that it is primarily within a society of low institutional differentiation and with flexible rôle-expectations that mysticism flourishes. If such a society is a society with few political channels, then mystics are being inclined towards social disengagement and moral passivity. If, however, the mystic happens to live in a society with many possibilities of political participation, then he or she might become more disposed towards moral and political actitivity.[13]

If Wuthnow is correct, then the relationship between mystical experiences and human behaviour is not an invariant one. This coincides with the findings of R.C. Zaehner in his book *Our Savage God* (1974).

It is not unlikely that this point could be generalized to other religious experiences, i.e. that there is no reason to believe that there exists invariant relationships between a certain kind of religious experience and a certain kind of human behaviour. The fruits of religious experiences are dependent upon a large number of factors besides the religious experience itself. And if this is the case, then it appears impossible to draw any conclusions concerning the veridicality of a religious experience from its fruits. If it is the case that a particular kind of religious experience in a certain type of situation leads to loving behaviour and an identical experience in another situation leads to moral passivity, then an application of the criterion of "fruits" would force us to say that the first experience is veridical, but not the second—although it is identical with the first! Assuming that the object of these experiences has not changed, it seems absurd to say that the first experience is veridical, while the second—identical with the first—is illusory.

Two things must, however, be remembered in the present context. First, it must be observed that it is one thing to advance a simplistic argument for the veridicality of a religious experience from its "good fruits". It is quite another thing to proceed on the assumption that a particular kind of experience *is* veridical and then to discern the general criteria (in a particular kind of situation) for the presence of such an experience. I would suggest that it is in this light that St. Paul's words to the Galatians could be understood: "The fruit of the Spirit is love, joy, peace, patience, kindness, goodness, faithfulness . . ." (Gal. 5:22). St. Paul presupposed the veridicality of certain spiritual experiences and discerned the fruits of those experiences. And he took the fruits of those experiences as a characteristic sign of the presence of the Spirit. This seems perfectly legitimate on the basis of its presuppositions.

Secondly, it is one thing to judge the *veridicality* of religious experiences from their fruits—it is quite another thing to judge their *value* from their fruits. And if it is the question of judging their value, then, surely, the fruits of the experience are of considerable importance. It is hard not to sympathize with William James, when he says:

If the *fruits for life* of the state of conversion are good, we ought to idealize and venerate it, even though it be a piece of natural psychology; if not, we ought to make short work with it, no matter what supernatural being may have infused it.[14]

Argument 2:—A human person might have an experience of God commanding a certain action, which is in clear conflict with a reasonable ethical judgement. The classical example of such a situation is God's command to Abraham to sacrifice his son Isaac. Is one justified in saying that Abraham's experience of God's command is illusory, because this command contradicts a reasonable ethical judgement (that it is wrong to hurt an innocent child)? A positive answer to this question might rest on the claim that God is good and because God is good God cannot (logically) issue commands which contradict reasonable ethical judgements. This argument seems decisive, but it could be evaded by the following move. It could be argued—as Kierkegaard did—that there are certain absolute duties to God which could indeed conflict with our duties to men. The only response possible to solve a conflict between these duties is to give our duties to God precedence before our duties to our fellow men. And the readiness towards such a response is clearly recognized by Genesis and Kierkegaard as a supreme act of faith.[15]

But it must be underlined that it could be recognized as such only in a situation where it was not evident—as it is in the New Testament—that God accepts duties to one's fellow men and women as duties to God's self. If this is recognized as a fact—and the authors of the New Testament urges us towards such a recognition—then it is the case that God has limited God's ways of testing the faith of God's people. It is a logical requirement for the story of Abraham and Isaac as a text of Abraham's faith, that Abraham did *not* recognize what is apparent in the moral teachings of the New Testament. If these moral teachings are recognized as true, then a trial of faith such as Abraham's cannot any longer be a trial of faith. In the light of the Christian revelation my response to an experience in which God commanded me to sacrifice my son could not possibly be any other than this: this command could not possibly be a command of God!

This does not imply that religious experiences of God commanding acts which strain our basic moral convictions can always be dismissed as illusory. It is not always easy to discern what is right and what is wrong and it is possible that there are religious experiences with illuminate persons about the will of God in such a way which is not in accordance with the moral convictions of many reasonable men and women. But even if our moral uncertainties sometimes make us unsure about the epistemological status of religious experiences, it is nevertheless "part of faith to hold that divine purposes and commands, *when more clearly understood,* will be shown to be good."[16] But we

137

might go one step further: if there is no evidence that such an understanding is forthcoming, then the judgement that the experience is illusory after all, is reasonable.

It must be underlined once again that such a moral critique of certain religious experiences will be justified only in the framework of a theology which accepts the basic presupposition that God accepts duties to our fellow-men and women as duties to God's self.

Argument 3:—In his famous book *Mysticism and Philosophy* (especially chapter 8) Walter Stace argues that mystical experiences provide a reason for loving behaviour. Stace does not—so far as I know—claim that this is a reason for regarding such experiences as veridical. But the argument developed by Stace could still be regarded as an important step in a larger argument to defend the veridicality of mystical experiences. Stace says:

> The basis of the mystical theory of ethics is that the separateness of individual selves produces that egoism which is the source of conflict, grasping, aggressiveness, selfishness, hatred, cruelty, malice, and other forms of evil; and that this separateness is abolished in the mystical consciousness in which all distinctions are annulled.[17]

Moreover, Stace argues that "mystical consciousness is the *only* source from which love flows into the world".[18] In the present context, however, we shall concentrate on the weaker claim that mystical consciousness provides a reason (there might be other) for the supreme value of love.

William Wainwright has argued against Stace's standpoint. The claim that there are no distinctions between selves and that human persons are fundamental identical, is *not* directly justified by mystical experiences.[19] There are—though Wainwright does not clearly stress this—two questions here:

1. is the unreality of all distinctions an intrinsic feature (i.e. not a result of a subsequent interpretation) of some sort of mystical experiences?
2. if the answer to 1 is yes, are we justified in concluding that it is in fact the case that all distinctions (especially those between human selves) are unreal?

In regard to question 1, Wainwright argues that the answer is no—and even if it was yes, mystical experiences would provide no reason for the value of love, since the presence of love presupposes difference and distance as well as union.[20]

When it comes to the second question, it is important to remember the discussion in chapter 8 about self-authenticating religious experiences. If there

138

are no such experiences—as we argued in chapter 8—then existence of mystical experiences, which have the unreality of all distinctions as an intrinsic feature, is not sufficient for concluding that it is in fact the case that all distinctions are unreal.

Argument 4:—Arthur C. Danto has made an impressive case for a position which is contrary to Walter Stace's; Danto claims that mystical experiences provide us with a reason for moral passivity. And he proceeds from a detailed theory about the relationship between factual beliefs and moral convictions. He summarizes his position on this issue in the following way:

> Whatever may be the logical connections between factual and moral propositions— and we assume that they are not the desired ones of entailment and deducibility— there is enough of a tie between them, so that when we reckon in the application conditions of moral beliefs, we have some basis for rational criticism and rational debate in the moral sphere.[21]

Given this point of departure, Danto presents us with the following question: do some significant types of religious experience present us with a view of reality which contradicts our basic moral conditions? And Danto answers this question positively. He claims that *monistic mystical experience* (experiences of reality as an undifferentiated unity)—as it has been fostered and relied upon by Indian philosophers—does provide us with a view of reality which deprives moral concepts of their application. Let us call this world-view *the amoral world-view*.

> The radical solution to the question: 'What ought we to do in the world?' is 'There is no world in which we can, much less ought to, do one thing rather than another'.[22]

William Wainwright has observed that R.C. Zaehner claims that a similar conclusion can be reached on the basis of the content of *cosmic mystical experiences* that opposites (including moral good and moral evil) coincide in the divine or ultimate reality. And Wainwright concludes that even if certain *interpretations* of monistic or cosmic experiences provide us with a reason for ethical nihilism, "these modes of consciousness are [not] *themselves* incompatible with a just appreciation of moral value".[23]

In a reply to Wainwright, Danto argues that it is difficult to tell where the line between the experience itself and its interpretation should be drawn.[24] This is, indeed, correct. But it is hardly a relevant remark since we have reason to believe that Danto's description of (monistic) mystical experiences (and Zaehner's description of cosmic experiences) do present us with interpretations of mystical experiences and not with the intrinsic features of such experiences. And the reason for this stems from the fact that there are other descriptions of similar experiences which do *not* imply that everything is an undifferentiated unity or that moral good and moral evil coincide in the divine. For example, scholars unanimously agree that Johannes Tauler denied the distinctionless unity between God and man in the mystical experience.[25] Further, Tauler understood the object of the mystical experience as a moral person.[26] Both these things—which are emphasized by Wrede —make it impossible to claim that Tauler was concerned with monistic or cosmic mystical experiences. The existence of such forms of mysticism warrants the conclusion that *it is far from obvious that monistic or cosmic mystical experiences present us with the intrinsic features of mystical experience.*

But Danto has another and more elaborate argument against Wainwright's claim that he has confounded certain interpretations of mysticism with mysticism itself. Danto argues that mysticism in general "seems to involve a transvaluation of values, or a devaluation of all values save those revealed to him at the high moment of insight, and he returns to a phenomenal world so transfigured, as virtually to be discontinous with the one he lived in before".[27] Danto's remark has a clear ring of truth, but one may question the relevance of his observation in the present context. No doubt, many mystics have been blinded by the overwhelming strangeness of their more or less sudden experiences. But the issue in the present context is not primarily about the psychological effects of the experience, but rather about the reason provided by the experience for affirming or denying an amoral world-view. Many mystics come to understand their experiences as an experience of the ultimate reality beyond good and evil. Thereby they may have found a reason for affirming an amoral world view. Other may understand their experience as an ineffable community with Supreme Goodness; like Tauler, they may then have found a supreme reason for an agapeistic way of life. The interpretative judgement of the experience rather than the experience itself, determines the possibility of finding reasons for or against a moral world-view. This is Wainwright's point; and I cannot see that Danto has been able to refute him.

The predictive criterion

There is another criterion of veridicality which is not so often discussed, but which still deserves to be mentioned in the present context. It has been underlined by a Swedish theologian, Hjalmar Sundén. He says:

> To have an experience is to be able to anticipate and make predictions. When we can make predictions about that which under certain conditions is going to happen, we consider ourselves to have made an experience. Perhaps we departed from an

experience of someone else, but when our prediction was verified, the experience of the other became our personal experience.[28]

Another Swedish theologian—Johan Unger—has claimed that experiential confirmation of an expectation cannot be a sufficient criterion of veridicality. Other criteria are needed.[29] This is surely correct. A certain experience may confirm our expectations—and still be an illusory experience. Some desert-travellers may expect to see an oasis in the desert. And they experience what they take to be an oasis. But it turns out that it is only a mirage. This shows that even if the mirage confirms our expectations we are not justified in taking it as a veridical experience. The experience of the oasis (which in fact is a mirage) creates new expectations—of water and relief—which upon further investigation turn out to be disconfirmed. Other desert-travellers are more lucky: they too expect to see an oasis—and when they see one their further expectations are confirmed by their subsequent experiences of water and rest.

These examples show that a predictive criterion must include a reference not only to the immediate confirmation of the expected experiences but also to the subsequent experiences. But can such a criterion be of any value in the field of religious experience?

Let me answer this question by reference to an important remark made by Wolfhart Pannenberg. He has suggested that a kind of predictive criterion became a dynamic factor in the Biblical history. He claims that there is an interaction between religious expectations and religious experiences in the testimony of Israel as told to us by the Biblical authors. The basis is a belief in God, who created heaven and earth, and the conviction that God chose Abraham and gave him the promise of the land of Canaan.

But the *understanding* of this promise has been transformed during the centuries under the impact of different historical experiences made by the people of Israel and their leaders. Against the background of the promise to Abraham, the escape from Egypt under the leadership of Moses was experienced as an act of God in the fulfilment of God's promises. But after the "promised" land was occupied there appears a gradual transformation of the understanding of God's promise. Obedience to the *Law* now becomes necessary if God's promise is to be sustained. God acts in history in order to punish Israel for its disobedience by letting enemies and natural disasters afflict the land. But God also rewards the people for their fulfilment of the law by prosperity and military victories. The Exile is an example of God's punishment. But God is also active in the acts of the Persian king Cyrus, which results in the liberation of Israel and their return to their former land.

During the Exile, there occurs, another transformation in the understanding of God's promises. The *final* fulfilment is now removed to the end of history,

141

when the Messiah shall restore Israel and the people shall be gathered on Zion. Under the influence of other experiences after the Exile a process is introduced which culminates in the beliefs of Jewish apocalyptics: God's final fulfilment of his promises is now removed to a state beyond history. And against this background the resurrection of Jesus is immediately perceived as an act of God, through which the goal of history (which is beyond history) is anticipated.[30] In sum: The crucial events in the history of Israel were (immediately or retrospectively) interpreted through the belief that God had given certain promises to the Fathers. But this belief also generated expectations about the future. And future events led them to revise their understanding of God's promises.

So, we may say that history taught the people of Israel an important religious lesson. Thereby we too may find a basis for a positive assessment of that religious tradition.

The intersubjective criterion

We shall conclude this chapter with a discussion of an important criterion. It is sometimes called the argument from unanimity.[31] Here we shall speak of the intersubjective criterion in order to bring out the continuity between this criterion and a principle which is operative in our commerce with empirical world. This criterion can be formulated in the following way: a religious experience is veridical if it occurs in different cultures and at different times. It is obvious, however, that some kind of elucidation of these general words is needed. The philosophy of science might give us a clue in this matter. Here some reference is often made to *the conditions under which an observation is made,* i.e. an observation is veridical if it is possible for every person who fulfills a certain set of conditions (is in possession of sufficient intelligence and necessary equipment etc.) to confirm the observation.[32] Similarly, we might say that—as a rule—a religious experience is veridical, if it is possible for every normal person who fulfils a certain set of conditions, to confirm that religious experience.

There are, at least, five influential objections against the idea of applying the intersubjectivity criterion in the field of religious experiences.

1. George Mavrodes has argued that it must be remembered that the object of most religious experiences is of a special character in comparison with the objects of sense experience. To the extent that the object of religious experience is a personal God, it should not be expected that experiences of God could be verified by any person who fulfils a certain set of conditions. God can be experienced only when God chooses to reveal God's self. God's will cannot

be compelled and "the failure of one person to apprehend God has very little significance against someone else's positive claim".[33]

This objection relies on the distinction between physical verification and personal verification. It is one thing to verify the existence or character of a person. It is another thing to verify the existence and character of a physical object. A person has a will of his or her own, but physical objects are "inert".

Still, I do not think that this distinction makes the idea of intersubjectivity in religious experience impossible. It may be the case that God can be experienced only when God chooses to reveal God's self. But at the same time it might also be the case that God has chosen to reveal God's self to those which are willing to fulfil certain conditions. The personal character of God is not incompatible with a certain "order" in the field of religious experiences. Similarly, human beings tend to reveal themselves to each other under certain conditions. If I am open, compassionate, attentative, loyal, sincere and respect the integrity and confidence of another person, then this person is more likely to "reveal" more of his or her self, than otherwise would be the case. Needless to say, there are no guarantees. I may have some hidden motives which are perceived by my partner and which blocks the process. Or my partner may have som special reasons for not "revealing" his or her self. But usually this is the way it works. Why should we not say something similar of God, if God is personal?

2. Another objection proceeds from the observation that the conditions for verifying religous experiences are variously described—and sometimes the descriptions seem contradictory. Some mystics advocate seclusion from the world, mortification of the body and other austerities. Other say that the important thing is to practice an agapeistic way of life in close communion with other men. Still others might argue that a certain kind of religious knowledge or insight is necessary. And the problem is not made easier by the fact that these recommendations are entwined with different religious world-views and confessional preferences.

There is, however, one basic thing in this context, which should be taken seriously. Everyone agrees that our cognitive capacity is dependent upon the broader context in which new knowledge is sought. Arthur I. Deikman has presented certain empirical evidence for the claim that there exists a particular mode of consciousness by which certain aspects of reality becomes accessible, which are not otherwise accessible. Deikman distinguishes between the receptive mode of consciousness and the active mode of consciousness. In the receptive mode the sensory-perceptual system is dominant. We concentrate on the perception of the environment rather than manipulation.

Other attributes of the receptive mode are diffuse attending, paralogical thought processes, decreased boundary perception, and the dominance of the sensory over the formal.[34]

The active mode—on the other hand—is manifested through "focal attention, object-based logic, heightened boundary perception, and the dominance of formal characteristics over the sensory: shapes and meanings have preference over colors and textures".[35]

I think that Deikman has given some ideas of how we might proceed towards some kind of greater consensus concerning the conditions for religious experiences. The different recommendations given by different religions need not be considered as contradictory, but rather as complementary. Meditation, prayer and other spiritual exercises can be seen as different ways to strengthen the receptive mode in an individual person. It is not necessary in this context to enter into a discussion about the pros and cons of these different methods.

3. But even if we reach some kind of agreement concerning the conditions which have to be fulfiled to prepare the ground for religious experiences, some sceptics would argue that an application of the criterion is far from fool-proof. Let us assume that the criterion works and that we are justified in claiming a certain intersubjectivity in religious experience. The experiences might still be illusions—only collective illusions. Walter Stace says:

> Even if all men had mystical experiences, instead of the almost infinitesimal proportion of men who now have them, and even if all these experiences were exactly alike, this would of itself show no more than that there is something in the nature of human beings, whether physical or mental, which makes them have these similar experiences.[36]

A similar argument is found in C.B. Martin's book *Religious Belief*.[37] And it is a serious argument. But we have to be aware of the context in which this argument is considered. If it is considered by itself as an argument to establish a necessary and/or sufficient criterion for the veridicality of religious experience, then we must admit that it does not work. But the situation is somewhat different if it is considered against the background of a metaphysics which has given us reason to affirm that a naturalistic world-view is not enough. This was the gist of the argument in the foregoing chapter. Adopting this perspective, less is required from the intersubjectivity criterion. We need some rules of thumb to distinguish veridical religious experiences. It is then quite natural to take note of the criteria which are used in experience in general and ask ourselves if these criteria can play a role in the religious field. We should not be surprised if some modification is needed. It is not possible to use these criteria without further ado. But it is still possible that they could give us some ideas about what is *characteristic* of veridical religious experiences.

4. What if the proposed criterion does not work? What if the suggested experiences do not occur? This is often taken as a starting-point to a refutation of the intersubjectivity criterion in religious experience. According to C.B. Martin:

> ... it is possible one should train oneself most assiduously in all of these ways and still not have truly religious experience. This possibility is characterized by saying that finally the favor and grace of God are required.[38]

And Jeffner concludes the argument (in a refutation of an argument by Price) by saying:

> To suggest a testing procedure that must be declared unworkable as soon as it fails to give the expected results is to suggest no testing procedure at all.[39]

But let us consider a clear case of personal verification. We may all agree about the claim that human beings are more likely to "reveal" themselves if they are treated as persons and not as things. A certain compassion, respect and sincerity is needed. Much more could be added about this. Still we all have experienced situations in which we think that we have done everything to "reach out" to another person—but we have failed to get anything back. Does this mean that we should leave the whole idea of reaching other persons by respect, compassion or sincerity? Or does it rather mean that we have been unable to fulfil the conditions for a personal relationship in an adequate way? I do not think it is irrational to claim that the fault lies with us and not with "the method" *if there exists sufficient evidence that the method has functioned in other cases.* And if such an attitude is rational in the field of human relations, why should it not be rational to take a similar attitude in the field of religious experiences?

5. Let us, finally, consider another argument against the religious use of the intersubjectivity criterion. We may admit that there are cases in which the criterion is defensible even if no religious experience appears. But what are we to say about the disagreements about the nature of the transcendent and particularly the disagreement between those who take the transcendent as personal and those who do not? It is obvious that different persons who have cultivated a receptive mode of consciousness still disagree about the nature of their experiences. How is this disagreement to be explained?

There are different possibilities here. First, it is possible that what they have experienced is so diffuse and unclear that their experiences could be interpreted in many ways. Some take it as an experience of a personal will and others as an impersonal principle or state. Secondly, it could also be the case that one group of witnesses—due to cultural influences—have drawn false conclusions from their experiences. Thirdly, it should not be ruled out that some kind of reconciliation is possible and that both parties may find reason to modify their contradictory descriptions.

A.C. Ewing has suggested that persons experiencing the transcendent as personal and persons experiencing the transcendent as impersonal, need to contradict one another. Their disagreement might be due to the fact that they have not experienced the same thing, or different aspects of the same thing. Ewing says:

> Perhaps the solution may be that we have here a conflict between two different modes of religious experience each with a different object. There might be a certain religious experience of the Whole such as the more characteristically mystical mystics have in high degree and also a religious experience of a personal or at least quasipersonal God who is part but not all of the Whole, and both experiences might be veridical without being incompatible with each other.[40]

To sum up: the intersubjectivity criterion cannot be used in the field of religious experience without considerable qualifications. The specific objects of religious experience must be considered. And even if some kind of agreement concerning the conditions of religious experiences can be reached, we are far from having a fool-proof criterion of veridicality. A religious experience can be veridical even if it does not satisfy the criterion—and a religious experience can be illusory even if it is universally available under certain conditions.

Nevertheless, it could be argued that even if it is neither a necessary, nor a sufficient condition of veridical religious experiences to be intersubjective, it is a characteristic of them to be so. This means that it would require a special explanation if a religious experience was veridical and not available for every normal human being, who fulfiled a certain set of conditions. The difficulty here is, of course, that such "special" explanations could be brought in whenever the expected experience does not occur: the special explanations, then, appear as a euphemism for "saving hypotheses". But the question is whether this verdict does full justice to the specific character of religion in general and Christian faith in particular: the restrictions imposed on the criterion of intersubjectivity in religion seems to follow from a concept of Deity which have many other sources other than the mere desire to salvage personal faith.

NOTES

[1] Mitchell 1958, p. 167.

[2] Broad 1953, p. 195.

[3] Broad 1953, p. 196.

[4] Hick 1983, p. 68.

[5] Hich 1983, pp. 70 f.

[6] See above in chapter 4, pp. 67—70.

[7] Jeffner 1966, p. 124.

[8] See for example Barr 1977.

[9] This conception of the "objective view" comes close to the position which Mitchell has termed "objectivism" in Mitchell 1980 b, pp. 31 f.

[10] Quoted by Holm in Holm 1979, p. 24.

[11] This depreciation of mystical experiences is also reflected in recent works on Christian doctrine by German-speaking theologians. See for Jeffner's analysis of this material in Jeffner 1977, esp. p. 69: "Es wäre zu erwarten, dass das reiche Erfahrungsmaterial der Mystik in diesem Zusammenhang positiv ausgenutzt würde. Das ist aber nicht der Fall. Alle Verfasser in unserem Material legen ganz im Gegenteil besonders Gewicht darauf, die akzeptablen Erfahrungen von den mystischen Erfahrungen abzugrenzen." It is also to be observed that mystical experiences has been of much more interest to English-speaking philosophers and theologians. See—for example—Broad 1953 and Stace 1960.

[12] Wuthnow 1978, p. 88.

[13] Wuthnow 1978, pp. 88 ff. See also Holm 1979, pp. 59 f.

[14] James 1974, p. 238.

[15] See Kierkegaard 1963 (Bind 5), pp. 63—74.

[16] Penelhum 1971, p. 311 (my italics)

[17] Stace 1961, p. 324. See also Wainwright 1976, pp. 30 f.

[18] Stace 1961, p. 327 (Stace's italics).

[19] Wainwright 1976, pp. 30 ff.

[20] Wainwright 1976, p. 31.

[21] Danto 1976, p. 24.—This view of the relationship between moral and factual beliefs is consistent even with an emotivist or prescriptivist theory of moral language. See Hudson 1970, p. 264.

[22] Danto 1976, p. 30. Compare this with the revealing words of Capra in Capra 1979: "The notion that all opposites are polar—that light and dark, winning and loosing, good and evil, are merely different aspects of the same phenomenon—is one of the basic principles of the Eastern way of life. Since all opposites are interdependent, their conflict can never result in the total victory of one side, but will always be a manifestation of the interplay between the two sides. In the East, a virtuous person is therefore *not one who undertakes the impossible task of striving for the good and eliminating the bad,* but rather one who is able to maintain a dynamic balance between good and bad." (p. 149, my italics).

[23] Wainwright 1976, p. 33.

[24] Danto 1976 b, p. 43.

[25] Wrede 1974, pp. 233 f.

[26] Wrede 1974, pp. 249 f.

[27] Danto 1976 b, p. 45.

[28] Sundén 1961, p. 35. See further Unger 1984, pp. 86 f.

[29] Unger 1984, pp. 86 f.

[30] Pannenberg 1961, pp. 91—95.

[31] See Stace 1961, p. 134.

[32] Bergström 1972, pp. 109 f. makes a reference to Feigl's contribution in Feigl & Brodbeck (eds.) *Readings in the Philosophy of Science* (1953), p. 11.

[33] Mavrodes 1970, p. 79.

[34] Deikman 1973, p. 69.

[35] Deikman 1973, p. 68.

[36] Stace 1961, p. 136.

[37] Martin 1967, p. 92.
[38] Martin 1967, p. 89.
[39] Jeffner 1972, p. 112.
[40] Ewing 1965, p. 17.

Bibliography

Abraham, W. 1982. *Divine Revelation and the Limits of Historical Criticism*. Oxford University Press. Oxford.

Alston, W. 1963. (Ed.) *Religious Belief and Philosophical Thought: Readings in the Philosophy of Religion*. Harcourt, Brace & World Inc. New York.

– 1964. "Psychoanalytic theory and theistic belief" in Hick, J. (Ed.) *Faith and the Philosophers*. Macmillan & Co. London. Pp. 63–102.

– 1967. "Religious language" in Edwards, P. (ed.) *Encyclopedia of Philosophy*. Vol. 3, pp. 168–174.

Baillie, J. 1939. *Our Knowledge of God*. Oxford University Press. London.

– 1965. *The Idea of Revelation in Recent Thought*. Oxford University Press. London.

Barbour, I. 1974. *Myth, Models and Paradigms*. The Nature of Scientific and Religious Language. SCM Press. London.

Barr, J. 1977, *Fundamentalism*. SCM Press. London.

Barth, K. 1961. *Church Dogmatics*. Selected by Helmut Gollwitzer; translated and edited by G.W. Bromiley. T. & T. Clark. Edinburgh.

– 1968. "Nachwort" in Bolli, H. (Ed.) *Scheleiermacher-Auswahl*. Siebenstern Taschenbuch. München & Hamburg. Pp. 290–312.

Becker, L. 1971. "A note on religious experience arguments" in *Religious Studies 7*, 1971. Pp. 63–68.

Bergson, H. 1935. *The Two Sources of Morality and Religion*. Translated by R.A. Audra and C. Brereton with the assistance of W.H. Carter. Doubleday & Co. Garden City (N.J.)

Bergström, L. 1972. *Objektivitet*. Prisma. Stockholm.

Berkeley, G. 1979. *The Principles of Human Knowledge*. (Ed. & Introd. by G. J. Warnock.) Fontana. Glasgow.

Braaten, C.E. 1966. *New Directions in Theology Today*. Volume II. History and Hermeneutics. The Westminster Press. Philadelphia.

Broad, C.D. 1953. *Religion, Philosophy and Psychical Research*. Routledge & Kegan Paul. London.

Brümmer, V. 1979. "Lyttkens on religious experience and transcendence" in *Religious Studies 15*, 1979. Pp. 221–225.

– 1984. *What Are We Doing When We Pray?* A Philosophical Inquiry. SCM Press. London.

Bråkenhielm, C-R. 1975. *How Philosophy Shapes Theories of Religion*. An Analysis of Contemporary Philosophies of Religions with Special Regard to the Thought of John Wilson, John Hick and D.Z. Phillips. CWK Gleerups. Lund.

Capra, F. 1979. *The Tao of Physics*. An Exploration of the Parallels between Modern Physics and Eastern Mysticism. Fontana/Collins.

Chisholm, R. 1966. *Theory of Knowledge*. Prentice Hall, Inc. Englewood Cliffs, N.J.

Christian, W.A. 1964. *Meaning and Truth in Religion*. Princeton University Press. Princeton (N.J.).

Copleston, F. 1977. *A History of Philosophy*. Vol. 9. Part I. The Revolution to Henri Bergson. Image Books. New York.

Cox, M. 1983. *Mysticism*. The Direct Experience of God. The Aquarian Press. Wellingsborough (Northamptonshire).

Danto, A.C. 1976. *Mysticism and Morality*. Oriental Thought and Moral Philosophy. Penguin Books. Harmondsworth.

— 1976 b. "Ethical theory and mystical experience. A response to professors Proudfoot and Wainwright" in *Journal of Religious Ethics 4*, 1976. Pp. 37—46.

Davidson, D. 1976. "Psychology as philosophy" in Glover, J. (Ed.) *The Philosophy of Mind*. Oxford University Press. Oxford. Pp. 101—110.

Deikman, A.J. 1973. "Bimodal Consciousness" in Ornstein, R.E. (Ed.) *The Nature of Human Consciousness*. W.H. Freeman and Co. San Fransisco.

Dionysios the Aeropagite. 1975. *The Divine Names and the Mystical Theology*. Translated by C. E. Rolt. SPCK. London.

Donovan, P. 1979. *Interpreting Religious Experience*. Sheldon Press. London.

Dostoevsky, F. 1945. *The Brothers Karamazov*. Transl. by C. Garnett. London.

Eckehart. 1955. *Deutsche Predigten und Traktate*. Herausgegeben und übersetzt von Josef Quint. Carl Hanser Verlag. München.

Ewing, A.C. 1965. "Awareness of God" in *Philosophy XL*, pp. 1—17.

Flew, A. 1966. *God and Philosophy*. Hutchinson. London. 1966.

Forell, U. 1968. "Kristen världsbild och vår erfarenhet" in *Insikt och handling*, 1968. Pp. 42—59.

— 1975. "Religiös erfarenhet i semantisk belysning" in *Årsbok för Kristen Humanism 1975*. (Ed. C.-H. Grenholm) Gummessons. Stockholm. Pp. 75—82.

Frankena, W.K. 1973. "Is morality logically dependant on religion?" in Outka, J. and Reeder, J.P. (Eds.) *Religion and Morality*. Doubleday. New York. Pp. 295—317.

Gilkey, L. 1961. "Cosmology, ontology and the travail of Biblical language" in *Journal of Religion 41*, 1961. Pp. 194—205.

— 1982. "God" in Hodgson, P. L. & King, R.H. (Eds.) *Christian Theology*. An Introduction to Its Traditions and Tasks. Fortress Press. Philadelphia.

Goudge, T.A. 1967. "Bergson, Henri" in Edwards, P. (Ed.) *Encyclopedia of Philosophy*, Vol. 1. Pp. 287—295.

Grice, H.P. 1968. "The causal theory of perception" in *The Philosophy of Perception*. (Ed. by G. J. Warnock) OUP. London. Pp. 85—112.

Görman, U. 1977. *A Good God?* A Logical and Semantical Analysis of the Problem of Evil. Verbum. Håkan Ohlssons. Lund.

Haikola, L. 1977. *Religion as Language-Game*. A Critical Study with Special Regard to D.Z. Phillips. CWK Gleerups. Lund.

Hamlyn, D.W. 1984. *Metaphysics*. CUP. Cambridge.

Hammarskjöld, D. 1980. *Markings*. Translated by W.H. Auden and Leif Sjöberg (with a foreword of W.H. Auden). Faber. London.

Hanson, U. 1973. *"Religious Experience"*. *En semantisk studie*. CWK Gleerups. Lund.

Happold, F. C. 1971. *Mysticism*. A Study and an Anthology. Penguin books. Harmondsworth.

Hare, R.M. 1958. "Religion and morals" in Mitchell, B. (Ed.) *Faith and Logic*. Oxford Essays in Philosophical Theology. George Allen & Unwin. London. Pp. 176—193.

Hay, D. 1979. "Religious experience amongst a group of post-graduate studentes—a qualitative study" in *Journal for the Scientific Study of Religion 18*. 1979. Pp. 164—182.

— 1982. *Exploring Inner Space*. Is God still Possible in the Twentieth Century? Penguin Books. Harmondsworth.

Hebblethwaite, B. 1980. *The Problems of Theology*. Cambridge University Press. Cambridge.
- 1976. *Evil, Suffering and Religion*. Sheldon Press. London.
Heidegger, M. 1953. *Sein und Zeit*. Max Niemeyer Verlag. Tübingen.
Helm, P. 1977. "Religious experience" in *Sophia 16*, 1977. Pp. 1–6.
Hempel, C. 1966. *Philosophy of Natural Science*. Prentice Hall Inc. Englewood Cliffs (N.J.).
Hepburn, R. 1966. *Christianity and Paradox*. Critical Studies in Twentieth Century Theology. Watts. London.
- 1967. "Religious experience" in Edwards, P. (Ed.) *Encyclopedia of Philosophy*. Vol. 3. Pp. 163–168.
Hick, J. 1964. "Theology and verification" in Hick, J. (Ed.) *The Existence of God*. Macmillan. New York. Pp. 253–274.
- 1966². *Faith and Knowledge*. Cornell University Press. Ithaca and London.
- 1968. "Religious faith as experiencing-as" in *Talk of God*. Royal Institute of Philosophy Lectures, Vol. 2 (1967–1968). Macmillan. London. Pp. 20–35.
- 1973. *Arguments for the Existence of God*. Macmillan. London.
- 1973². *Philosophy of Religion*. Prentice Hall Inc. Englewood Cliffs (N.J.).
- 1974. *Evil and the God of Love*. Collins. The Fontana Library.
- 1977. "Comments on Penelhum" in Coward, H. & Penelhum, T. *Mystics and Scholars*. SR suppl. 2. Calgary. Pp. 83 f.
- 1983. (with M. Goulder). *Why Believe in God?* SCM Press. London.
Holm, N.G. 1979. *Mystik och intensiva upplevelser*. Publications of the Research Institute of the Åbo Akademi Foundation. Åbo.
Hospers, J. 1946. *Meaning and Truth in the Arts*. The University of North Carolina Press. Chapel Hill.
Hubbeling, H.G. 1981. *Einführung in die Religionsphilosophie*. Vandenhoeck & Ruprecht. Göttingen.
Hudson, W.D. 1970. *Modern Moral Philosophy*. Macmillan. London.
- 1974. *A Philosophical Approach to Religion*. Macmillan. London.
- 1975. *Wittgenstein and Religious Belief*. Macmillan. London.
- 1979. "The concept of divine transcendence" in *Religious Studies 15*, 1979. Pp. 197–210.
- 1983. Review of Swinburne's *Faith and Reason* (1981) in *Religious Studies 19*, 1983. Pp. 93–96.
Ivanka, E.V. 1964. *Plato Christianus*. Uebernahme und Umgestaltung des Platonismus durch die Väter. Johannes Verlag. Einsiedeln.
James, W. 1974. *The Varieties of Religious Experience*. A Study in Human Nature. Fontana. London.
Jeffner, A. 1966. *Butler and Hume on Religion*. A Comparative Analysis. Diakonistyrelsens bokförlag. Stockholm.
- 1972. *The Study of Religious Language*. SCM Press. London.
- 1977. *Kriterien christlicher Glaubenlehre*. Almqvist & Wiksell. Uppsala.
- 1977 b. "Livsåskådningsforskning—material och metoder" in Holte, R. (Ed.) *Livsåskådningsforskning*. Almqvist & Wiksell. Uppsala.
- 1979. "The relationship between English and German ways of doing philosophy of religion" in *Religious Studies 15*, 1979. Pp. 247–256.
- 1981. *Vägar till teologi*. Verbum SKEAB. 1981.

Jørgensen, T.H. 1977. *Das religionsphilosophische Offenbarungsverständnis des späteren Schleiermacher.* J.C.B. Mohr (Paul Siebeck). Tübingen.

Kasper, W. 1980. "The Augsburg confession in Roman Catholic perspective" in *The Augsburg Confession in Ecumenical Perspective* (Ed. by H. Meyer). LWF Report. Geneva. Pp. 163–187.

Katz, S. 1978. "Language, epistemology, and mysticism" in Katz, S. (Ed.) *Mysticism and Philosophical Analysis.* Sheldon Press. London.

Kennick, W.E. 1967. "Ineffable, The" in Edwards, P. (Ed.) *Encyclopedia of Philosophy,* vol. 3. Pp. 181–183.

Kierkegaard, S. 1963. *Samlede værker. Bind 5–6.* (Udgivet av A.B. Drachman, J.L. Heiberg og H.O. Lange.) Gyldendal. Köbenhavn.

Lossky, V. 1957. *The Mystical Theology of the Eastern Church.* James Clarke & Co Ltd. London.

Lyttkens, H. 1979. "Religious experience and transcendence" in *Religious Studies 15,* 1979. Pp. 211–220.

Körner, S. 1984. *Metaphysics: its Structure and Function.* CUP. Cambridge.

Marc-Wogau, K. 1945. *Die Theorie des Sinnesdaten.* Probleme der neueren Erkenntnistheorie in England. Lundequstiska bokhandeln. Uppsala.

Martin, C.B. 1967. *Religious Belief.* Cornell University Press. Ithaca, New York.

Mascall, E. I. 1958. *He Who Is.* A Study in Traditional Theism. Longmans, Green & Co. London.

Mavrodes, G. I. 1970. *Belief in God.* A Study in the Epistemology of Religion. Random House. New York.

– 1978. "Real vs. deceptive mystical experiences" in Katz, S. (Ed.) *Mysticism and Philosohical Analysis.* Sheldon Press. London.

McPherson, T. 1974. *Philosophy and Religious Belief.* Hutchinson. London.

Miles, T.R. 1972. *Religious Experience.* Macmillan. London.

Mitchell, B. 1958. "The grace of God" in Mitchell, B. (Ed). *Faith and Logic.* Oxford essays in philosophical theology. George Allen & Unwin. London.

– 1970. *Law, Morality and Religion in a Secular Society.* Oxford University Press. London.

– 1980. "Does christianity need a revelation? A discussion [together with Maurice Wiles]" in *Theology,* march 1980, Pp. 103–114.

– 1980 b. *Morality: Religious and Secular.* The dilemma of the traditional conscience. Clarendon Press. Oxford.

– 1981. *The Justification of Religious Belief.* Oxford University Press. New York.

Moore, J.M. 1938. *Theories of Religious Experience.* With Special Regard to James, Otto and Bergson. Round Table Publ. New York.

Moore, P. 1978. "Mystical experience, mystical doctrine, mystical technique" in Katz, S. (Ed.) *Mysticism and Philosophical Analysis.* Sheldon. London.

Nagel, E. 1956. *Logic without Metaphysics.* And other Essays in the Philosophy of Science. The Free Press. Glencoe (Ill.).

Niebuhr, H.R. 1960. *The Meaning of Revelation.* Macmillan. New York.

Nielsen, K. 1973. *Scepticism.* Macmillan. London.

Nordenfelt, L. 1974. *Explanation of Human Action.* Philosophical Studies published by the Philosophical Society and the Department of Philosophy. University of Uppsala, Sweden. Uppsala.

Nygren, A. 1960. *Essence of Christianity.* Two Essays. Translated by Philip S. Watson. Wiliam B. Eerdmans Co. Grand Rapids (Mich.).

- 1966. *Eros and agape*. Den kristna kärlekstanken genom tiderna. Aldus/Bonniers. Stockholm.
Oakes, R.A. 1972. "Is 'self-validating' religious experience logically possible?" in *The Thomist 36*, 1972. Pp. 256–266.
- 1976. "Religious experience and rational certainity" in *Religious Studies 12*, 1976. Pp. 311–318.
- 1979. "Religious experience, self-authentication, and modality *de re*: a prolegomenon" in *American Philosophical Quarerly 16*, 1979. Pp. 217–224.
- 1981. "Religious experience, sense-perception and God's essential unobservability" in *Religious Studies 17*, 1981. Pp. 357–367.
Origen. 1965. *Contra Celsum*. Translated with an introduction & notes by Henry Chadwick. Cambridge University Press. London.
Otto, R. 1925. *Das Heilige*. Ueber das Irrationale in der Idee des Göttlichen und sein Verhältnis zum Rationalem. Gotha Leopold Klotz Verlag. Leipzig.
Pannenberg, W. (et al.) 1961. *Offenbarung als Geschichte*. Vandenhoeck & Ruprecht. Göttingen.
- 1962. *Was ist der Mensch?* Vandenhoeck & Ruprecht. Göttingen.
- 1967. *Grundfragen systematischer Theologie*. Gesammelte Aufsätze. Vandenhoeck & Ruprecht. Göttingen.
Pears, D. 1971. *Wittgenstein*. Fontana/Collins. London.
Penelhum, T. 1971. *Religion and Rationality*. An Introduction to the Philosophy of Religion. Random House. New York.
- 1977. "Unity and diversity in the interpretation of mysticism" in *Mystics and Scholars*. The Calgary conference on mysticism. Ed. by Harold Coward and Terence Penelhum. Canadian Corporation for Studies in Religion. Supplements 3. Pp. 71–81.
Pettersson, O. 1966. *Afrikas religioner*. Svenska Bokförlaget Bonniers. Stockholm.
Pettersson, T. 1975. *The Retention of Religious Experience*. Almqvist & Wiksell. Stockholm.
Phillips, D.Z. 1970. *Faith and Philosophical Enquiry*. Routledge & Keagan Paul. London.
- 1970 b. *Death and Immortality*. Macmillan. London.
Pike, N. 1970. *God and Timelessness*. Schoken Bookes. New York.
Price, H.H. 1964. "Faith and belief" in Hick, J. (Ed.). *Faith and the Philosophers*. Macmillan. London. Pp. 3–25.
Ramsey, I. 1957. *Religious Language*. An Empirical Placing of Theological Phrases. SCM Press. London.
Russell, B. 1967. *History of Western Philosophy*. And its Connection with Political and Social Circumstances from the Earliest Times to the Present Day. George Allen & Unwin. London.
Schleiermacher, F. 1927. *Werke*. Auswahl in vier Bänden. Dritter Band. Felix Meiner Verlag. Leipzig.
- 1958. *Ueber die Religion*. Reden an die Gebildeten unter ihren Verächtern. Verlag von Felix Meiner. Hamburg.
Schlesinger, G. N. 1983. *Metaphysics*. Methods and Problems. Basil Blackwell. Oxford.
Shepard, J. 1975. *Experience, Inference and God*. Macmillan. London.
Singleton, W.F. "Teilhard on Camus". Unfortenately, I have lost the reference to the journal in which this article was published.

Smart, N. 1960. *A Dialogue of Religions*. SCM Press. London.
- 1972. *The Concept of Worship*. Macmillan. London.
- 1978. "Understanding religious experience" in Katz, S (Ed.). *Mysticism and Philosophical Analysis*. Sheldon Press. London. Pp. 10−21.
Smith, J. 1968. *Experience and God*. Oxford University Press. New York.
Stace, W. 1961. *Mysticism and Philosophy*. Macmillan. London.
- 1969. *Time and Eternity*. An Essay in the Philosophy of Religion. Princeton University Press. New York.
Sundén, H. 1940. *La Theorie Bergsonienne de la Religion*. Almqvist & Wiksell. Uppsala.
- 1961. *Människan och religionen*. Verbum. Stockholm.
Sutherland, S. 1977. "St. Paul's Damascus Experience" in *Sophia 16*, 1977, vol. 2. Pp. 8−17.
- 1984. *The Concept of Revelation*. Unpublished lecture at the 5th European Conference on Philosophy of Religion in Lund.
Swinburne, R. 1974. *The Existence of God*. Clarendon Press. Oxford.
Taylor, A. 1970. "Two proofs of God's existence" in Mavrodes, G. I. (Ed.). *The Rationality of Belief in God*. Prentice Hall. Englewood Cliffs (N.J.).
Teilhard de Chardin, P. 1975. *Le Milieu Divin*. An Essay on the Interior Life. Collins. Fontana Books. London.
Tillich, P. 1964. *Systematic Theology. Vol 2*. James Nisbet & Co Ltd. Digswell Place.
Unger, J. 1976. *On Religious Experience*. A Psychological Study. Almqvist & Wiksell. Stockholm.
- 1984. *Gudsupplevelse*. Den religiösa erfarenheten och rollteorin. Proprius förlag. Stockholm.
Wainwright, W.J. 1973. "Mysticism and Sense Perception" in *Religious Studies 9*, 1973, Pp. 257−278.
- 1973 b. "Natural explanations and religious experience" in *Ratio 15*, 1973. Pp. 98−101.
- 1976. "Morality and Mysticism" in *Journal of Religious Ethics 4*, 1976. Pp. 29−36.
- 1978. *Philosophy of Religion*. An Annotated Bibliography of Twentieth-Century Writings in English. Garland Publ. Inc. New York.
Ward, K. 1982. *Rational Theology and the Creativity of God*. Basil Blackwell. London.
Wiles, M. 1974. *The Remaking of Christian Doctrine*. SCM Press. London.
- 1976 b. *What is Theology?* Oxford University Press. London.
- 1980. "Does christianity need a revelation? A discussion [together with Basil Mitchell]" in *Theology*, March 1980. Pp. 103−114.
Wisdom, J. 1965. *Paradox and Discovery*. Basil Blackwell. London.
Wittgenstein, L. 1966. *Lectures & Conversations on Aesthetics, Psychology and Religious Belief.* (Ed. by Cyril Barrett.) Basil Blackwell. London.
- 1969. *Tractatus Logico-Philosophicus*. Routledge and Kegan Paul. London.
Wrede, G. 1974. *Unio Mystica*. Probleme der Erfahrung bei Johannes Tauler. Almqvist & Wiksell. Stockholm.
Wuthnow, R. 1978. *Experimentation in American Religion*. Berkeley.
Yandell, K. 1977. "Self-authenticating religious experience" in *Sophia 16*, 1977. Pp. 6−17.
Zaehner, R.C. 1957. *Mysticism; Sacred and Profane*. An Inquiry into Some Varieties of Praeternatural Experience. Clarendon Press. Oxford.

Index of persons

156

Index of subjects

157